JUST AROUND THE CORNER

The Paradox of the Jobless Recovery

STANLEY ARONOWITZ

JUST AROUND THE CORNER

The Paradox of
the Jobless Recovery

TEMPLE UNIVERSITY PRESS PHILADELPHIA

Stanley Aronowitz is Distinguished Professor of Sociology at the Graduate Center, City University of New York, and editor of Temple University Press's *Labor in Crisis* series.

Temple University Press
1601 North Broad Street
Philadelphia PA 19122
www.temple.edu/tempress

Text design by Kate Nichols

♾ The paper used in this publication meets the requirements of the American National Standard for Information Sciences—Permanence of Paper for Printed Library Materials, ANSI Z39.48-1992

Library of Congress Cataloging-in-Publication Data

Aronowitz, Stanley.
Just around the corner : the paradox of the jobless recovery / Stanley Aronowitz.
p. cm.
Includes bibliographical references and index.
ISBN 1-59213-137-9 (cloth : alk. paper)—ISBN 1-59213-138-7 (pbk. : alk. paper)
1. United States—Economic policy.   2. United States—Economic conditions.
3. Unemployment—United States—History—20th century.   4. Labor—United States.
5. Income distribution—United States.   I. Title.
HC103.A8   2005
330.973—dc22
2004055303

2 4 6 8 9 7 5 3 1

CONTENTS

PREFACE

I N THE EARLY 1990s William DiFazio and I coauthored a book called *The Jobless Future*. It represented the outcome of almost a decade of research and reflection about the consequences of the latest technological revolution for the U.S. economy, especially prospects for jobs. We visited industrial workplaces and institutions where the computer embodied the main means of material and knowledge production. We conducted a fairly large series of interviews and ethnographic observations of scientists as well as computer people, managers, and workers. We took these experiences seriously but also valued the theoretical and contemporary work of other researchers. In contrast to the prevailing common sense we insisted on the separation of the concepts of paid work and jobs. "Paid work" may be offered on a contingent, part-time, or temporary basis. This form of employment is almost commonplace in the retail sector but is increasingly being used by businesses that want maximum flexibility in hiring and firing qualified knowledge workers. In most contemporary universities, for example, adjuncts are hired on a semester basis and enjoy no assurance that they will return the next semester, or the next year. Similarly, many Microsoft contract employees have no benefits; while their pay is higher than those with Microsoft jobs, they are subject to termination when their contracts expire. Employees who have jobs, unlike paid workers, presume some assurance that unless business is slack, they stay on the payroll and have health insurance, paid holidays and vacations, and pension benefits.

We concluded that new technologies such as computer-mediated material production, information gathering and dissemination, and entertainment do not make work disappear, but that the prospects for jobs and job growth were dim. We predicted that computers and automation would enable fewer workers to produce more goods, so manufacturing jobs would steadily diminish in the absence of growth in the Gross Domestic Product beyond the historical annual average of less than 3 percent in material production and in knowledge. But our most controversial statement was that, on the basis of our analysis, professional, technical, and scientific labor would also be affected. Contrary to some who claimed that technological change invariably created more jobs than it destroyed, this era of technological transformation would reverse the historical trend; no less than production labor, knowledge work—done by computer programmers, systems analysts, technicians, and eventually engineers—would produce more but offer fewer job opportunities. In other words, the irony of knowledge production is that it displaced its own jobs as well as those of others. We saw the beginning of the well-known transformation of the full-time job with benefits and a degree of security to part-time, temporary, and contingent labor among the most highly qualified workers, including professors. And we noted that the globalization of production would have a lasting effect on the U.S. workplace.[1]

Throughout the late '90s our thesis was widely denied, even scorned, by celebrants of the "new economy." These soothsayers foresaw a recession-free economy for the era, albeit one that would witness the replacement of manufacturing with a generation of "symbolic analysts"—highly educated knowledge workers whose high salaries would more than compensate for the loss of well-paid union production jobs. Based on this claim, the steady two-decade bleeding of more than nine million production jobs in America's industrial heartland was virtually ignored, except in business pages. That the vaunted employment of financial-services personnel also suffered erosion in the midst of a stock-market surge escaped their notice. What they did see, and incessantly hyped, was the dot.com boom that, for the length of the decade, hired tens of thousands of computer people to develop and disseminate the new information technology of the Internet, the proliferation of the personal computer, and the conversion of many economic sectors—especially, but not exclusively, the wholesale and retail trades—to computer-based sales, accounting, bookkeeping, and industrial production.[2]

Needless to report, the 2000–2 recession and the accompanying, more profound dot.com bust sobered the wild and unsupported prognostications of the technophiles, even as thousands of small firms failed and tens of thousands of qualified computer professionals were laid off. But despite the evidence of a "recovery" without commensurate job growth, as the economy picked up in 2003–4 they resumed their mantra that we should remain calm, even as three million more industrial jobs disappeared. As I show in this book, they hold fast to the same neoliberal doctrine that dominates official government and business circles: the conventional wisdom that technological change produces more jobs than it destroys. In the current environment of sluggish job growth, we

have seen some of the same experts rehearsing their now questionable arguments. Moreover, as I argue in Chapter Three, what the
economists and many politicians count as jobs are of the contingent
kind, so-called McJobs. But *Just around the Corner* does not rest
content to debunk, disparage, and deconstruct. It offers reasons
why we have arrived at a historic crossroads, and a program for addressing our chronic problems. Neither *The Jobless Future* nor this
book takes the position of the technophobes. Although we show
the dire consequences of technological displacement in a society
with huge holes in its safety net, we forcefully argue that technology that eliminates the most physically brutal, mind-numbing
and health-endangering forms of labor is a good thing, provided
workers share the benefits of greater productivity, so that it is genuinely "labor saving" and not "labor destroying." And we insist
that technological innovation be accompanied by a tight safety net.
We insist on the imperative for creating jobs that expand our public
goods. DiFazio and I proceeded from John Kenneth Galbraith's
argument that public squalor amidst private wealth is unaccept-
able for a country as rich as ours. In an era of privatization and
further gutting of our already enfeebled public goods, Galbraith's
admonition is even more urgent today.[3] As I show in Chapter Six,
if we can afford a half trillion dollars or more every year in military expenditures—whose job-creating impact has been diminished because of technological change—we can create millions of
labor-intensive jobs to provide education, child-care, health, environmental, and public-recreational services. We can spend public
money to encourage farmers to produce genuinely organic food,
and we can provide comprehensive and exhaustive inspection of
our seriously endangered food supply. We have the resources to
develop alternative energy resources to oil and coal. Equally important, we need to openly acknowledge the limits of the concept
of full employment in an evolving economic regime dominated
by technoscience and, specifically, the limits of the concept of the

full-time job. We suggest that workers in the new economy need shorter hours. On this shift we need to ask questions about the concentration of wealth and power.

I have tried to compress my analysis into a concise essay. Along the way I have accumulated some debts. Ellen Willis and my editor, Micah Kleit, read the entire manuscript and made detailed suggestions; Bill DiFazio's approbation was very important to me. And I want to thank my Labor and Social Theory Seminar in spring 2004 at CUNY Graduate Center for criticism, questions, and comments on some of these ideas.

INTRODUCTION

ECESSION, Recovery, the market, profit taking, Dow Jones
and NASDAQ averages, GDP, joblessness, factory orders, the
Consumer Confidence Index. The phrases tumble out of television, radio, and newspaper reports like a waterfall. Many viewers,
readers, and listeners often feel they are drowning in business jar-
gon. What do these terms mean, and what does their movement
signify for the economy, for our jobs, for our income? Most of
us can make only vague sense of these abstractions, yet they are
the fare of everyday news. Is the information conveyed by highly
charged economic terms meant to shape our perceptions or to
sharpen our understanding? Is the business news, as some critics
charge, not about the specifics of the economy, but about selling
the virtues of the prevailing economic system and reassuring the
perplexed that all is well? How much do most of us really know
about how the economy and finance really works? For example,

when we learn from the newspaper, online Web sites, television, or radio business reports that the unemployment rate has "dipped" from 6 percent to 5.9 percent, the one-tenth of 1 percent drop is almost never translated into numbers. How many people does 6 percent represent? To answer this question one needs to know the size of the nonfarm labor force. Do the announcers supply this information? What does a tenth of a percent drop really signify in relation to broad trends? Aside from its effect on the laid-off worker, does the gain or loss of twelve thousand jobs mean all that much for a labor force of 120 million? Besides, if the tenth of a percent drop in the unemployment rate resulted from the withdrawal of workers from the labor force rather than from an increase in jobs, is it good for the economy, or for those still looking for work?

Conversely, suppose stocks lose value even if unemployment drops and there is more work for the jobless. When factory orders dip but the Dow gains, reporters and commentators often remark that the "market shrugged off" the bad news. But if the Dow lost some "points," the same commentators might attribute this event to the "disappointing" news about industrial activity. And what are we to make of the frequent relationship between layoffs announced by a firm and a dramatic jump in its stock price? Why do investors like a firm that proves to be a relentless cost cutter? If the Dow Jones Index rises coincident with the lowered jobless rate, is this movement a cause-effect relationship or might there be other factors that account for the rise? Will investors even discount the significance of employment gains if they fear inflation that might prompt rising interest rates?

Not so long ago business news was confined to the business pages, far from the purview of all but investors, economists, and professional managers. Today, newspapers like the *Wall Street Journal* and the *Financial Times*, a British business publication, are as likely to adorn the breakfast table as the local news daily. And to compete with the "trade" papers, national newspapers such as the *New York Times*, the *Washington Post*, and the *Los Angeles Times* have expanded their business sections. Mergers and acquisitions, bankruptcies, business scandals, and dramatic changes in stock quotations are as likely to land on their front pages as a presidential speech, political news, or gossip about the latest Hollywood or pop-music star. What has changed?

One explanation for the ubiquity of business news is that many Americans have become small investors. They have replaced savings accounts with stock portfolios. Millions of Americans now have equity in stocks and bonds and, for this reason, are likely to follow the business news carefully, at least the fate of the firms they have put their money on. With the expansion of private pensions, often in the form of mutual funds, Americans have suddenly discovered they have a "stake" in the system, let alone the stock-and-bond markets. The incentive to pay attention is increased because the money managers who control the mutual funds frequently offer individual accounts over which the member has some discretion among a limited menu of options.

For example, a college professor earning a relatively modest salary whose supplementary pension is tied up in one of the largest of these funds with several million subscribers, Teachers Insurance Annuity Association (TIAA), may have accumulated hundreds of thousands of dollars during the stock-market boom of the 1990s, if she chose to invest her money in relatively risky stocks rather than in the safer but less remunerative bonds and Treasury bills. She might have put some portion of her annuity account into real estate and "social" investments, and another percentage into the stock market. Since these programs are composed of funds contributed by both the subscriber and the institution that employs her, it is not unusual over twenty or thirty years for her to have achieved a retirement income, including Social Security, that exceeds her salary. During the peak of the boom, subscribers' supplementary retirement annuities were enough to prompt a good number to retire well before the age when they were eligible for Social Security benefits.

Lunchtime conversations in many workplace cafeterias revolve as much on the latest gyrations of the Dow or of a particular firm as they do on sports or campus gossip. If in the late 1990s some who had heavily invested in stocks gloated over their good fortune, in the past three years such conversations resembled a collective wailing wall as the Dow took a nosedive and, before it hit bottom in early 2003, lost a third of its price; reflecting the so-called dot.com bust, the NASDAQ—the main technology exchange— lost 60 percent. Some who had hoped for early retirement were forced to postpone their plans. A fifty-seven-year-old woman who had hoped to retire early now says she will never retire because she lost so much of her savings during the 2000–2002 bust. Others of retirement age clung to their jobs and transferred their depleted funds to safer bonds and treasury bills. A third group, which had bought houses and apartments that depended on the inflated investment prices or projected retirement income, were obliged to sell their real estate, sometimes at bargain prices.

Another reason for the expanded interest in business news is that in the 1970s, perhaps more than at any time since the post– Civil War era, the United States seemed to have entered a new Gilded Age. Once again, the "business of America is business." In the late nineteenth century industrial and financial tycoons were virtual folk heroes, presidents of the United States were considered by the voters as little more than servants of big business, and the two main political parties brazenly competed for favors from the high and the mighty—leaders of Wall Street and the steel and food trusts of Pittsburgh and Chicago. This is once more a time of overarching business dominance, not only of the mechanisms of political and economic power, but over the hearts and minds of a considerable portion of the American people.

Even as the gap between rich and poor widens, and journalists and academics analyze the "disappearance" of the middle class, Americans watch with awe and wonder as millions of the best working-class factory jobs evaporate and computer programmers and analysts vainly search for work after the collapse of the dot.com boom. But many of the system's victims forgive even when they don't forget, because they believe that one day they, too, shall reap the spoils of America's unparalleled wealth. Rather than rise up in anger, many have displayed infinite patience as they wait for that wonderful day to arrive. More to the point, if they have experienced bad fortune, they believe they have only themselves to blame, not their employers or the economic royalists who have made "business ethics" an arcane term.

That the CEO and other top officers of the Enron and WorldCom Corporations presided over the pillaging of employee-pension funds while drawing millions in salary and perks detains us not at all; even the workers who have watched their hard-earned pensions melt are mostly hoping for some restitution. Few have taken to the streets or to the media to protest; while there are court suits, most employees have prudently refrained from condemnation or from threatening massive legal action against the perpetrators. Laments like "the road not taken" and "if only I had listened" ring in the ears of the disappointed. The view that small investors should shun the stock market and put their money into safer, if less lucrative, bonds or Treasury bills is today termed foolish by investment counselors who promise their clientele that if they can hold out by absorbing sometimes daunting losses, the market will inevitably turn for the better. And, of course, this is little more than a truism. After two years in the doldrums, in summer 2003 the Dow began to climb once more—strengthened, according to some experts, by the faith of small investors. Many who took the heaviest losses in the 2000–3 recession and stock-market fall have become convinced that, despite the catastrophe, they have little choice but to reach for the fast buck, the main chance, and the part of the American dream that ignores the harsh reality: In broad terms, few of us will ever get rich or even accumulate a small fortune. For the awful truth is that "small" signifies that the investor has few, if any, resources to weather the troughs of market behavior.

In sum, in a culture that still celebrates the rags-to-riches myth, the stock market has become the middle-class lottery of choice, and the typical small investor has as much chance of making a genuine fortune as any player has of winning the lottery. The lottery bettor risks relatively little when he stands in line at the corner drug- or grocery store and buys a five-dollar ticket. The difference between the two is that millions have, intentionally or not, placed their pension money in the roller coaster we call the "market" in hopes that they get out with their nest egg intact before the inevitable crash.

Conventional economic wisdom took heavy blows in 2003.

By statistical measures—the growth in the production of goods and services in the domestic economy—government officials and corporate economists announced that America came out of a very short-lived recession in November 2001. According to the logic, economic growth eventually translates into more jobs. But from the perspective of job creation, official unemployment statistics seemed to belie the fact of recovery. Two years after government officials and private economists declared a turnaround, official joblessness hovered around 6 percent, or eight million unemployed. Somehow Americans did not believe the forecasters. "Even though the recession ended nearly two years ago," wrote *New York Times* reporter Steven Greenhouse on September 1, 2003, "polls are showing that American workers are feeling stressed and shaky this Labor Day." Citing the 2.7 million jobs lost over the previous three years—one million of them since the "recovery"—Greenhouse quotes a number of labor economists, one of whom says that "American workers are doing very badly." From where the workers stood in most regions, including the South, which had shrugged off previous recessions, jobs were hard to find. A staple of the regional economy, textiles, had for the past five years joined the exodus of many apparel jobs to Mexico and especially to China.[1]

The story of the migration of Huffy, the world's largest bicycle producer, tells an important part of the story. Five years ago, one thousand unionized Huffy workers put in their last day of work at the company's Celina, Ohio, plant after city and county officials failed in their bid to keep the company from pulling up stakes to move to nonunion Farmington, Missouri, where employees were paid $2.50 less an hour than Celina's $10.50 average wage. Still labor costs were too high, at least compared to Nuevo Laredo, Mexico, just across the Rio Grande from Texas, the company's next move. There, workers were paid half the wage of Farmington workers. Two years later the company "cut its ties to Mexico and began importing its bikes almost entirely from China, where workers earn less than 4 percent of what Huffy paid in Celina," or about forty cents an hour.[2]

Still, in his 2003 Labor Day appearance before what Greenhouse described as a "subdued" audience of skilled Ohio union workers, President George W. Bush insisted that the economy was getting better and worker productivity was rising, even as he acknowledged the apparent disconnect between the (weak) economic growth and rising unemployment. Moreover, unlike previous periods, during the more than two years of statistical recovery between fall 2001 and the end of 2003, jobs continued to disappear. Less than a week after Bush's speech the federal Department of Labor announced that although official joblessness had declined one-tenth of 1 percent in August, contrary to economic forecasts that predicted a modest rise of twenty thousand jobs for the month, the economy lost ninety-three thousand jobs.

How to explain the paradox of sluggish but upward growth of the Gross Domestic Product (GDP) and declining official unemployment amid job losses? Continuing a long-term trend, more than a hundred thousand workers left the labor force in September because they gave up their futile job search. So the total nonfarm labor force—defined by the Bureau of Labor Statistics as those who are working for wages and salaries or are actively looking for work—was smaller, and the percentage of workers seeking paid labor declined slightly. Once again the slippery statistical measures tend to conceal more than they reveal.

On December 6, *New York Times* business writer Louis Uchitelle reported:

> The nation's employers displayed an unexpected reluctance in November to hire more workers despite the improving economy and rising demand for what they sell.
>
> Several weeks of bullish economic reports raised expectations that hiring, at long last would break out of the doldrums. Corporate profits rose sharply in the third quarter. Construction spending is up. So are car sales, and consumer spending, after a brief dip, has picked up as well. Overall, the government estimate of economic growth in the third quarter was revised up by a full percentage point last week to 8.2 percent at an annual rate.
>
> But chief executives have held back on hiring, concerned that the third quarter surge would turn out to be an anomaly. . . . Forecasters surveyed by Blue Chip economic indicators agree with the executives: their consensus estimate of economic growth in the fourth quarter is 3.6 percent at an annual rate.
>
> "There is no question that company managers are trying to squeeze every ounce they can from the existing employees before they give in to hiring," said Nariman Bahravesh, chief economist at Global Insight, a data gathering and forecasting service.[3]

To be fair, October and November witnessed modest job growth. But results hardly justified the cautious official optimism: In contrast to the 1990s recovery when employment rose 225,000 a month for nearly seven years, in the last six months of 2003, economist Paul Krugman stated, "less than 90,000" new jobs a month were added, "even below the 150,000 jobs needed to keep up with the growing working-age population."[4] But as Jared Bernstein of the Economic Policy Institute observed: "The number and quality of the jobs we are creating are still insufficient to sustain a truly robust recovery," because many are in low-wage service industries and reflect the growing importance of temp agencies in the employment market. Most of the 150,000 "jobs" added in October were temporary and highly contingent. More than 100,000 of them were "self-employed contractors,"[5] often a euphemism for former employees of companies which, having cut them loose from their pension and health benefits, continued to employ them as contract workers. Some of these jobs were offered on a part-time basis. In contrast to Europe where time unemployed is calculated in the statistics, according to U.S. labor statistics, any part-time employment counts as full-time when unemployment is measured. And November's 51,000 new jobs, the quality of which remained largely unreported, was sharply below predictions. Meanwhile manufacturing employment continued its long-term slide despite the end-of-year report that new factory orders had increased. All told during the last five months of 2003, as the Bush administration crowed about the recovery, just 278,000 new jobs were created, an average of a little more than 55,000 a month.

We should expect economic growth in the wake of "military" Keynesianism, where public investment, but not in social services, becomes the engine of capital accumulation in production and service industries, and in employment. This type of investment assists the private sector and, in the shadow of rising budget deficits, usually entails stagnation or deep cuts in public spending for health, education, housing, and even veterans' services, unless an administration is prepared to borrow heavily to maintain public services. Thus, like Ronald Reagan in the 1980s, Bush turns out to be one of the great "big spenders"; only when the Democrats are in the White House do conservatives invoke the doctrine of balanced budgets and other fiscal constraints. Contemporary conservatism is committed to reductions of public goods and privatization of the remainder, transfer payments from the public till to large corporations, and tax cuts for the rich—all of which entail, but only implicitly, that the bill will be paid by the 90 percent of the population that struggles to make ends meet.

In stark contrast to its free-market ideology, taking a page from Ronald Reagan's playbook, the Bush administration, with congressional approval, pumped almost a half-trillion dollars of military spending into the economy during 2003 and proposed to pour billions more in 2004 and 2005 into a new initiative to colonize Mars. Corporations that benefit from accelerated defense contracts—those who make weapons, textiles, or clothing and build facilities and companies that deliver the raw materials; firms such as Halliburton and Bechtel, which have received huge contracts for Iraq reconstruction; and companies that develop and produce software and hi-tech security equipment—have generally reported higher profits, and their shares in the equities markets have risen as well. Yet merchants across the country said the Christmas shopping season, which came on the heels of the announcement that Congress had approved an unprecedented $487 billion military budget was, with the exception of luxury items, not especially successful; the small rises in revenues were "disappointing."[6] It appears that "middle-class shoppers" were still worried about mounting job losses and, consequently, refrained from ebullient buying.

Were the modest gains in consumption due primarily to an anxiety-ridden public's irrational fears of joblessness? Perhaps the tepid Christmas 2003 buying season was rooted in a realistic assessment of the economic situation. Consider the lively 8.2 percent third-quarter growth in 2003. On the eve of the buying season, hourly wages rose by a mere two-tenths of 1 percent, but when inflation is factored in, real wages actually declined by three-tenths of 1 percent. This means that whatever gains were made did not benefit the more than 80 percent of the workforce whose income was essentially stagnant. Pop-ups on the computer screen, billboards, and TV and radio ads tell a story of a significant part of the population saddled with stagnant wages and drowning in debt. The ads are for firms that promise to help individuals consolidate their debt by, in some cases, helping them to accumulate more debt (at astronomical interest rates). There might be a boom in the debt-consolidation industry and certainly in high-interest finance companies, but most consumers did not feel the recovery.

The bombshell was delivered early in January 2004. Defying predictions by the administration and most independent economists that December's data would show a 150,000-job growth, the economy added just 1,000 jobs as the unemployment rate declined by two-tenths of 1 percent, a sign that more workers had left the labor force. Some accepted early retirement "in a lean job market," as Louis Uchitelle reported, often leaving good jobs in their fifties despite their recognition that almost none of the pension packages companies offer are enough to live on without supplementary income, and despite their uncertain prospects for finding another job. The *Financial Times* commented that December's job performance cast doubt on the recovery, and citing a number of economists, *New York Times* commentator Edmund Andrews indicated that the Bush administration had run out of options. Poised to raise interest rates on the certainty that the economy was picking up, the Federal Reserve, which had sought to boost growth by lowering them to 1 percent, seemed to have no place to go. Andrews concluded that Bush could only wait.[7]

ESPITE DRAMATIC GAINS following World War II, the rewards of growth and the advent of consumer society were distributed unevenly throughout the U.S. economy. The vicissitudes of capital investment, corporate decisions concerning plant relocation (partly to escape high union labor rates), shifts in energy resources, and technological innovation conspired to widen the gap between rich and poor and between growth and decline. In the midst of the astounding productivity of the agricultural sector, rural communities went into a tailspin from which most have never recovered. From the 1920s through the 1960s, the internal migration of black and white farmers from the South and other leading rural areas to the cities matched the volume of people who immigrated to the United States during the forty years of the turn of the twentieth century. More than forty years ago, presidential candidate John F. Kennedy discovered rampant poverty in the coal-mining areas of the Appalachian mountains—West Virginia, Kentucky, parts of southwestern Pennsylvania, and Tennessee—and growing unemployment in New England owing to the migration of cotton and wool mills to the Southeast. Although Congress had passed "depressed areas" legislation in 1958, the 1960–61 recession deepened the crisis beyond the resources provided by the existing law. An important component of Kennedy's presidential campaign and his first year in office was to address "pockets of poverty" by pouring billions into public works, job training, and income maintenance in these regions. These measures provided a model for the Economic Opportunities Act, which extended public services, income support, education, and job training to major urban areas, where capital flight and southern migration to the cities had produced a festering field of discontent and potential insurgency.

The insurgency that emerged in many black communities from coast to coast began in 1964, even as the Johnson administration vigorously pursued the contours of Kennedy's antipoverty legacy, because, while there was federal commitment to address the issues of urban and rural unemployment, the administration hesitated to provide funds for the expansion of public goods. With the exception of health and elementary education, in the end Johnson's Great Society antipoverty program relied on the private sector to provide jobs for the unemployed. Until America's growing involvement in the Vietnam War, upon which 1960s economic growth depended, this strategy remained more effective at the rhetorical than at the material level.

But macroeconomic trends show only one side of the real jobless crisis. Like the late 1950s and early 1960s when Americans began to wake up to the "depressed areas" problem—the scandalous condition of poverty amidst prosperity—we are currently rediscovering the need to "dis-aggregate" unemployment statistics to find out what is really happening to local communities. A comprehensive report by the Employment Policies Institute on the "local unemployment crisis" for 2002 lists 397 counties and cities with populations greater than ten thousand, totaling more than twenty-six million, whose jobless rates are 9 percent or higher. The unemployment rates range from a high of 25 percent in Maverick County, Texas, to 9 percent in Barbour County, West Virginia. Many counties in California, Texas, Ohio, and Illinois never came out of the recession. And the Southeast—particularly Alabama, North and South Carolina, and Mississippi—registered double-digit unemployment rates, reflecting the exodus of textile mills in the past three years. Only New Jersey among the northeastern states has most of its major cities with more than 10 percent joblessness, although Rochester, New York; Detroit, Michigan; Cleveland, Ohio; Dallas, Texas; Portland, Oregon; and Bakersfield and Modesto, California—among the largest cities in their respective states—have 9 to 12 percent of their official labor force out of work.[8]

This situation points to the danger of basing economic evaluations on abstract categories like the Gross Domestic Product, aggregate unemployment statistics, or investment data. These measures hide the unevenness of decline and recovery. As I shall argue in Chapter Two, the real problem is that conventional economics does not take into account the complexity and the novelty of the current situation. Although jobless recoveries are no longer unique—indeed the 1991–93 recession exhibited similar characteristics—many communities are suffering more than others. Moreover, the nature of "jobs" has changed. In this book, I will not consider labor or work a real job unless it possesses the following minimum characteristics:

- There is a presumption of *permanence*. Thus, when economic conditions justify layoffs due to slack orders, the employer is committed to calling the worker back when business picks up.
- The job entails *benefits* such as health care, pensions, paid holidays, and vacations.
- Even in nonunion workplaces the employer recognizes that there is, in effect, an informal contract that under ordinary business conditions protects the worker from arbitrary discharge and in matters of promotion. In fact, one of the major spurs to union organization is the failure or refusal of the employer to acknowledge this contract.

In sum, a "job" as opposed to "work" entails genuine protections and perquisites. At the turn of the twenty-first century, in the name of "flexibility," millions of workers are condemned to temporary, part-time, and contingent employment. But unlike the 1990s when employers in almost every sector of the economy put this labor regime in place, there is no longer plenty of work and almost no new jobs. Many jobs are being transformed into contingent positions, and even these contingent positions are disappearing faster than new hires are being created.[9]

Just as the coal regions of southeastern Kentucky and northeastern manufacturing centers such as Newark, New Jersey, actually lost jobs during the relatively robust growth of the late 1950s and 1960s, so—largely due to the long-term migration of traditional jobs from the North and Midwest—cities like Cleveland, Rochester, and Detroit were left behind in the hi-tech boom of the 1990s. The case of Rochester, a leading manufacturing center for cameras and electronic equipment such as photocopying machines, was especially painful. The city's major corporations, Eastman Kodak and Xerox, as well as nearby IBM, underwent major restructuring and decentralization of their manufacturing facilities during this period. Thousands of well-paying jobs were exported from the region, and neither federal nor state economic-development programs were able to fill the huge holes left by the exodus. For this was the time of budget balancing, budget cuts, and significant tax breaks by local governments to large industrial corporations, including Kodak. The company accepted the incentives to stay in town but eventually took the money and ran. If President Bush remained anxious for news, by the end of January 2004 there was new cause for hope and despair.

On January 25, the Job Market section of the *New York Times* reported some hiring in industries besides tourism. Its illustrative example: the huge Wall Street firm Merrill Lynch, which "had cut thousands of jobs since 2000," indicated it would hire 650 financial analysts during 2004. Trucking and some manufacturing employers said they had similar hiring plans. Some might argue that while new hiring was still relatively sluggish, this was encouraging news. But neither Bush nor the employees and citizens of Rochester, New York, rejoiced when Eastman Kodak revealed plans to lay off some fifteen thousand employees worldwide by 2006, about seven thousand in the Rochester area. The company, which once employed sixty thousand workers in Rochester and a quarter million worldwide, has steadily reduced its global and local workforces to a third of their size twenty years ago. In Buffalo, New York, once an important steel, metalworking, and chemical center whose leading plant, the huge Bethlehem steel mill in adjacent Lackawanna, closed in the late 1990s, thousands of single-family homes were abandoned by workers who were forced to leave the region in search of work. The city government took the houses over and offered to give them away to anyone who showed the ability to rehabilitate and maintain them.[10]

The difference between now and the 1960s and early 1970s is that political will has evaporated to address the problems faced by cities like Rochester and Buffalo. The reasons are not hard to fathom: In the first place, there is little visible protest against onerous economic conditions that have left thousands permanently jobless; in the second place, since the early 1970s, occupants of the White House from both major political parties have adopted neoliberal economic doctrine and renounced the earlier Keynesian policies of public job creation and long-term income supports for the chronically unemployed and underemployed introduced during the New Deal, which were still in effect until around 1973. As a result, aside from responding to intense pressure to extend jobless benefits for thirteen or more weeks on the expectation that the "recovery" will eliminate the emergency, neoliberal policy refuses to put in place any program dedicated to job creation; the federal government may incur a deficit to expand the military in times of war, but under no circumstance will it replicate civilian Keynesianism. Indeed, in 1996, Democratic President Bill Clinton signed welfare-reform legislation designed to end the fifty-year-old program under the assumption that the basic reason people suffer chronic unemployment is personal, not economic.

This book will argue that our country is facing structural joblessness that we can expect will resist real accumulation of goods and services. Joblessness already affects segments of the population that have not suffered structural unemployment since the Great Depression—industrial workers; managerial, professional, and technical occupations; and service employees. In the next chapters I discuss and account for the befuddlement of most economists and politicians, offer a broad picture of how the economy works in this age of global capitalism, provide an explanation for the jobless "recovery," offer alternatives to the bankrupt religion of the free market, and offer a political analysis of how the grave situation facing us may be overcome.

ONE

HOW WE GOT HERE

*A Snapshot Economic History
of America*

WE AMERICANS ARE NOT KNOWN for our long memories. Two generations after the beginning of the ten-year Great Depression, we seemed to have forgotten its crucial lesson: Unfettered free markets for speculative investment are a formula for mass unemployment, human misery, and even starvation. The Reagan Revolution that exuded the optimism of the late 1920s also brought a message of disdain for the idea of public goods, including Social Security, federal aid to education and health, and the public Medicare program. It was—in the words of the Michael Douglas character in what was perhaps the iconic film of the 1980s, *Wall Street*—a moment when the dominant business ethic was "Greed is good." Amid the pronouncements of the Reagan administration against "big government," his was an era of profligate public spending on the military. But the 1990s witnessed a historical reversal of political roles. The Democratic

Clinton administration was relatively tight-fisted and fiscally prudent. Like Franklin Delano Roosevelt's key platform plank in the 1932 presidential campaign, Clinton promised—and delivered—a balanced budget.

In a collection of his *New York Times* columns, the intrepid economist Paul Krugman reflects on the first three years of the administration of George W. Bush and calls it "The Great Unraveling." His pieces are a long string of complaints and condemnations of the Bush economic policies: unwarranted tax cuts, mainly for the rich; consequent huge budget deficits; corporate scandals without swift government action; bad management of the 2000–2002 recession; and other calumnies which, as a staunch Democrat, Krugman ascribes to the president's lack of fiscal moderation and his administration's disregard of the fundamentals of public policy. In Krugman's estimation, despite fierce partisan criticism, the Clinton administration's economic policies in contrast improved the lot of most Americans:

> First and foremost for the lives of most people by the end of the 90s jobs were plentiful, more plentiful than they had been for decades. . . . If job growth was impressive the increase in productivity—the amount produced per worker—was even more impressive. In the 1970s and 1980s low productivity growth—barely 1 percent a year—was the greatest failing of the US economy. . . . But during the 1990s productivity took off; by decade's end it was rising faster than ever before in American history, and wages had ended their long stagnation.[1]

Krugman does not credit the Clinton administration directly with creating jobs (job creation is not on the neoliberal table), increasing productivity, and the slowing of wage raises that kept profits high. The implication is that Clinton's bold initiative to raise taxes against the prevailing religion of "No new taxes" that had sunk the previous Bush administration; his consistent pursuit of balanced budgets, largely by means of chopping federal jobs, reducing some benefits programs, and "ending welfare as we know it"; and an internationalist foreign economic policy, especially in the wake of the Mexican and Japanese crises, generated an optimistic economic environment that produced admirable results.

From its inception in early 2000, Krugman's twice-weekly column was avidly followed by *Times* readers, and within months of its appearance, he became the darling of liberals and the Left for his uncompromising attacks, not only on the Bush economic policies, but also on the administration's conduct of the Iraq war and its disturbing civil-liberties record. We may remain skeptical that the 1990s were a golden age for the postwar U.S. economy. But Krugman's invocation to recent U.S. economic history is consistent with a position widely held in centrist and left-liberal circles.

The Bush administration—which, it may be argued, drove the Reagan "revolution" to its logical conclusion, a place that Reagan himself was wary to go—represents a sea change in national economic policy and, according to Krugman's lights, the Clinton administration was the apex of sound, conservative government economics that led to a new era of now interrupted prosperity. Like Reagan's, and despite its antigovernment and austerity rhetoric, the Bush administration has proven to be one of the biggest spenders in peacetime history. The ballooning arms budget has combined with the two huge tax cuts to place this administration in league with the deficits incurred by the New Deal during the Great Depression. Under the Far Right leadership of John Ashcroft, its Department of Justice imposes government surveillance on dissenters and, on its broad interpretation of the war on terrorism, sanctions federal-agency intrusion into the private life of any U.S. citizen; Bush has repeatedly called for privatizing Social Security and, in the guise of providing a prescription benefit for seniors, in fall 2003 pushed through Congress a program to privatize significant portions of Medicare.

Throughout his commentary, Krugman has made an important if inadvertent point: In the post–Cold War era the Democrats are the real fiscal conservatives. In the 2004 presidential-primary season, nearly all the main contenders for the Democratic Party's presidential nomination railed against Bush's fiscal profligacy and his love affair with corporate "special interests" such as Enron and other energy corporations and with the Wall Street inside traders and lashed their favorite whipping post, Vice President Dick Cheney's former company, Halliburton, which aggrandized from the administration nearly $9 billion in noncompetitive federal Iraq reconstruction contracts. They did not hesitate to accuse the Bush administration of squandering the "Clinton surplus" on tax cuts (to which some candidates added an unjustified steep rise in military spending).

Borrowing a chapter from the Republican conservatives' book, it was Clinton who balanced the budget and actually left a surplus upon his retirement from the presidency. The surplus was produced not primarily with tax increases but with extremely prudent spending. Under Al Gore's direction, the administration cut federal payrolls by 10 percent and held the line on spending for new education, health, and veterans' programs. While the Republican attack ads never hesitated to accuse the Clinton administration of "tax-and-spend" politics and trotted out a long string of "welfare cheats" as living testimonials to the degeneration of the New Deal and its legacy, Clinton—not his predecessors George H. W. Bush, Reagan, or Richard Nixon—signed the Welfare Reform Act in 1996 and pursued its implementation with exceptional vigor. The legislation, which put a five-year limit on income support and required recipients to enter minimum-wage "work" programs as a condition of retaining their benefit, was perhaps the most dramatic assault on the poor since the Hoover years. With a stroke of the pen, it abolished the only guaranteed-income program in U.S. history.

What Clinton proved in his eight presidential years is that even if, since the end of the Cold War, the two parties are somewhat divided on international economic and military policy, neoliberal free-market policies are the bipartisan economic hallmark of the post–Cold War era. The difference is that, under the guidance of the centrist Democratic Leadership Council, founded by Clinton in 1988 to bury the remnants of New Deal welfare policies, the Democratic Party and its candidates are more firmly committed to fiscal austerity than is the Right. In fact, Clinton's triumph was so complete that none, including the "liberal" wing of the Democratic Party, dare utter its name or articulate the traditional New Deal welfare-state policies, except in their desiccated forms— supporting universal health care managed by private insurance companies; making the labor law somewhat more protective of worker rights, but not challenging the so-called free speech of employers; linking income assistance to the long-term unemployed to make-work requirements; keeping the federal bureaucracy small, regardless of how it affects such vital services as inspections and oversight of food, drugs, and other consumer protections; and maintaining business and environment regulation, but mainly on a voluntary basis.

We cannot understand this apparently strange turn of events, let alone the paradox of the jobless recovery, unless we have a clearer grasp of U.S. economic history. For, if many are perplexed by Bush's decisive turn to military Keynesianism, which entails deficit spending and dramatic debt accumulation, a brief examination of the century and half since the Civil War might help put these changes in perspective. What we shall find is that in stark contrast to the traditional claim that the United States never had

an empire because it held few colonies, militarism is no stranger to
U.S. history. And, contrary to the prattle of free-market capitalism,
the state has long been joined at the hip with big business. What
may come as a surprise to some is that there never was a free
market—if by this term we mean that government corresponds
to Adam Smith's metaphor of a night watchman: a state whose
principal function is to defend the nation's geographic borders,
to issue currency, and to protect private property, but that strictly
eschews economic intervention. In reality, the activist state knows
no particular political party. Republicans as much as Democrats
have recognized their responsibility to aid business achieve profitable investments in material ways, and this includes manipulating
and otherwise influencing markets.

In truth, there is a substantial body of political and intellectual
opinion which viewed it as the fundamental business of government to provide the infrastructure of roads, communications, and
other public goods to facilitate economic growth even before the
New Deal, and to create public financial institutions such as the
Federal Reserve Bank to stimulate private investment through regulation of interest rates when the market fails to provide sufficient
incentives. We will also discover that war, whatever its origins in
politics, is a prime mover of economic growth and of technological
innovation. In this respect, the Bush administration conforms to
the historical pattern of U.S state economic policy more than de-
viates from it. In sum, if there is blame to be fixed, while there are
individuals who can be pinned with the tag of corruption and other
villainies, in most cases they are following a structural, systematic
drift of U.S. political economics. To account for our current dilem-
mas, we must go deeper than the practice of demonization, which
can only mask the roots of the current crisis. We may find that, as
James Truslow Adams once argued, our business civilization itself
is our problem rather than a few bad apples who operate within it.

of private wealth, also witnessed the emergence of a new labor movement. While unions trace their history to the U.S. colonial period, and in selected cities such as New York, Philadelphia, and Boston the ante-bellum working-class movement had made both a political and economic difference, it was not until the 1870s with the formation of the Knights of Labor that a national labor movement was organized. A decade later, the American Federation of Labor brought together disparate craft unions in a single federated organization. Even as its leaders insisted that only skilled trades workers were capable of self-organization, at a time when they were subject to ten- and twelve-hour days and wages that were barely adequate to bring them back to work each day, production as well as craft workers in steel, apparel, and textiles responded to what became the most notable AFL campaign, the struggle for the eight-hour day. In the 1890s, under the dynamic leadership of Eugene V. Debs, later to become the perennial Socialist presidential candidate, railroad workers organized a national industrial union—a term that signifies that skilled and unskilled belonged to the same organization. The American Railway Union staged a major national strike against a group of employers who were the literal personifications of the robber barons. At the same time, skilled and unskilled workers at the Homestead mill of the Carnegie Steel Corporation struck against wage cuts prompted by the introduction of new steel-making technologies that rendered some crafts obsolete.[7]

The first two decades of the new century, dubbed the "progressive" era by labor and social historians, were years of protest and reform, interrupted briefly by the U.S. entry into the World War. From the alliance of an insurgent labor movement and progressive reformers against child labor; the fight to enact health, housing, and factory-safety legislation; the radical-led textile strikes in Lawrence, Massachusetts, and Patterson, New Jersey, in 1912 and 1913; and the AFL's successful organizing effort in meat packing and the textile strike of 1919 to the first great national strike in the history of the industrializing era, which involved unskilled and skilled workers from more than fifty nationalities in steel, the moment had come when the steady march of capital was finally challenged.

Perhaps the most complex legislation of this era was the Sherman and Clayton Acts, 1892 and 1913, respectively. Under the slogan "antitrust," these measures were designed to slow, if not reverse, the growing concentration of capital in America's major economic sectors. They attempted to regulate the widespread practices of price-fixing, patent sharing, and technology suppression, consequences of the centralization of ownership in fewer hands. In the early 1900s, companies such as U.S. Steel Corporation, Standard Oil, General Electric, Allied Chemical, Dupont, and Union Carbide were the giants of their respective sectors. There were four leading meat-packing corporations, who set the prices and controlled the technology and distribution routes for the entire industry. Sherman notwithstanding, these corporations retained the lion's share of their respective markets into the 1930s, when, during a brief revival of progressivism, Congress and the administration of Franklin Delano Roosevelt attempted to enforce and improve the antitrust legislation. But despite the widespread antibusiness sentiment among the general public, much of it fueled by the Great Depression and the consequent upsurge in mass labor unionism, against the bitter opposition of the giant trusts, Roosevelt's trust buster, Thurman Arnold, and Congress's leading progressive, Robert LaFollette, were able only to expose the violations of free enterprise and business competition by the giant monopolistic corporations. They succeeded in imposing some new regulatory laws to curb their worst practices, but the concentration of capital rolled on.

The railroads were only the beginning of the communications explosion. By World War I, with the assistance of federal and state regulatory agencies, every mass-production industry employed electricity to power machines, and electricity lit most urban households and retail establishments. The commercial development of the telephone, telegraph, automobile, and airplane, also under federal regulation, not only revolutionized everyday life but also brought into being entirely new industrial groups. These corporations, based in the auto, electrical, telephone and telegraph, and energy industries, did not, except for the motorcars, rely on traditional crafts. And the auto assembly line made craftspersons into maintenance mechanics, who were now semi-skilled instead of production workers. They introduced a new element into industry—scientific and technological knowledge; raised the significance of the once independent occupations of engineer and scientist; and brought into existence a whole new layer of technicians. Even as the Ivy League and other leading private colleges and universities remained centers of undergraduate teaching and liberal scholarship, industrial, mechanical, electrical engineering, and other technological fields became crucial to the mission of public higher-education institutions, notably New York's City College, Cornell University, the University of California, and the so-called land-grant universities such as Wisconsin, Michigan, and other Midwest state universities founded after the Civil War to provide expertise for the development of agricultural and mechanical technologies.

Like the periodic waves of immigration that began with the Puritans, the United States has always relied on a steady stream of "foreign" labor at all levels of education and skill. Having locked down five million blacks in the semi-feudal and repressive regime of Southern plantation agriculture after the Civil War, Northern capital soon ran out of native-born unskilled and semi-skilled labor for the burgeoning production, mining, and transportation industries. Just as the British and Irish economic slump of the 1840s had provided a coterie of skilled and unskilled workers for the growing

U.S. textile mills and its busy seaports, and as the failed 1848 revolution in Germany drove legions of skilled workers to America's
machine-tool factories and iron foundries, the neat coincidence
of the late nineteenth-century world agricultural crisis provided
a solution for the labor shortages in mass-production industries.
Again the federal government complied, this time by opening the
nation's borders to millions of eastern and southern European immigrants, many of whom became the core labor forces in mining,
iron and steel, textile, and apparel industries, mainly in the Northeast and Midwest. Later, as the need for labor subsided and in the
wake of the pre– and post–World War I labor upsurge, especially
in steel and textiles, during which many of the newly arrived immigrants from Italy, Poland, Russia, and other eastern European
countries played leading roles, in 1920 Congress approved new,
restrictive immigration laws that effectively thwarted the dreams
of many Europeans.

But laws that placed restrictions and established quotas on entry did not halt the stream of immigrants. Corporate agriculture
required seasonal laborers, who after the Great Depression could
not be recruited from the native born; the hotel and restaurant
industries routinely employed immigrant labor; and as the apparel
and shoe industries went global after 1960, domestic factory owners went underground: They continued to employ undocumented
Asian, Mexican, and Caribbean immigrant labor, often at submin-
imum wages, in cities such as New York and Los Angeles. Neither
the McCarran anti-immigration legislation passed at the height
of the McCarthy era nor the best efforts of the Immigration and
Naturalization Service, which operated the border-policing activities, were adequate to halt the steady stream of undocumented
immigrants who by 2003 numbered some fourteen million, not
only from Latin America but also from Asia and the Caribbean.
Reflecting the apparently unstoppable tidal wave of immigration
in his January 2004 State of the Union address, President Bush

announced a proposal to grant the immigrants "guest worker" status. Emulating a longtime practice in European countries and the relatively short-lived bracero program in the United States after World War II, the proposal recognizes the fact of illegal immigration and tacitly acknowledges its indispensability to many low-wage industrial and service sectors. At the same time, Bush made clear that his administration did not favor granting the immigrants citizenship, a prohibition that would enable the authorities to import and deport workers as the economic situation and the political climate dictated.

The 1920s were poster years for the American Century. There was a general consensus among nations and commentators that the United States had established both economic and political dominance in the world. After a wartime interlude of unprecedented federal economic intervention—to guarantee a high level of military equipment, but also to purchase labor peace by recognizing, selectively, the right of labor to organize and bargain collectively with employers—at home, laissez nous faire returned with a vengeance. Reacting to the national steel strike, in 1919 Woodrow Wilson's attorney general, A. Mitchell Palmer, took the occasion to raid radical offices and meetings, arresting thousands of immigrants and, after kangaroo-court proceedings, deporting some 2,500 labor and radical activists to their native lands. As a new Republican president took office, in 1921 and 1922 in swift strokes, leading employers in meat packing, textiles, rail, and steel lashed out mercilessly against labor strikes and organizing efforts. Conservative Republican administrations quickly removed wartime business controls. By 1926, the pace of growth of industrial production began to flag; by 1928 it was already in decline, and, signaled by a series of bitter strikes in clothing, textiles, and mining against employer-imposed wage cuts, wages began to sink rapidly. Millions lost their jobs as employers adjusted their sights to flagging demand. But during these years, the unregulated stock market maintained a dizzying pace based almost entirely on speculation; the prices of stocks were wildly out of kilter with the so-called fundamentals: the value of plant and machinery, profitability of the production enterprises, the size of the actual market for goods, and the level of new investment in machinery and labor.

Seventy-five years after the fact, there is no consensus concerning the cause of the economic crisis that turned America and the world upside down. The mainstream economists and historians point to unregulated speculation, which in a "free" market would inevitably need to correct itself downward—the more inflated stock prices in relation to the fundamentals, the steeper the fall. There are still those who insist that both the Hoover and Roosevelt administrations moved too quickly to intervene and thereby permanently distorted markets for capital, goods, and services.[8] Some have argued for a version of an underconsumption thesis: Too many goods found too few buyers. As goods piled up in warehouses, there were few incentives to produce more, and layoffs invariably followed.[9] But there was little doubt that the halcyon years of the 1920s—which witnessed the introduction of a mass credit system amidst falling or stagnant wages and widespread technological changes that displaced labor in the wake of economic stagnation and led to burgeoning industrial production—came crashing down when profit rates in the manufacturing sector began to fall, unsold inventories rose, and, as a result, mass layoffs occurred. When these did not solve the problem of overproduction and falling profits, many employers and small farmers were driven into bankruptcy. Those that survived were forced to mortgage their farms and capital to banks and insurance companies, which in turn found themselves holding worthless stock and mortgage paper.

The 1929 stock-market crash delivered a powerful blow to at least one staple of the prevailing free-market ideology: that left to itself the market would achieve a balance between production and consumption, profits and wages. In the United States, the level of adjustment was way below full employment because the ideology of market freedom was here the most extreme. Under Herbert Clark Hoover's administration the federal government simply refused to provide a floor under wages in forms such as unemployment insurance and relief, and the labor movement was divided on the issue of federal intervention and besides was extremely weak. The worldwide Depression of the 1930s hit no advanced industrial country harder than the United States. By 1932, more than a quarter of the labor force was officially unemployed, but many progressive analysts calculated the figure at more like a third, or seventeen million workers. Unlike Britain, where a coalition Labor-led government initiated a program of relief for the unemployed, President Herbert Clark Hoover urged private charities such as religious institutions to take major responsibility for providing food, clothing, and other forms of aid to the poor.[10]

However, even as he urged an acceleration of private giving, Hoover barely hesitated to heed business demands that the government step in to save their dwindling stock of capital, much of which had gone up in the smoke of the stock crash. Working within the classic trickle-down, supply-side doctrine revived in the 1980s, Hoover authorized the organization of institutions such as the Reconstruction Finance Corporation to provide low-interest business loans as a means to stimulate investment and offered tax relief to stricken employers. By these means, Hoover hoped that prosperity would resume. Economists, Democrats, and the voters concluded that Hoover's efforts were too little and too late and threw him from office. Americans were ready for change, and the core of their demand was a mainline injection to put people back to work or to provide federal income support for the large fraction of the population that was falling or had already sunk into poverty.

Although the New Deal was to retain and expand much of Hoover's approach in the National Industrial Recovery Act,

strengthening bank and commerce regulation and adding intervention into the farm sector—measures explicitly sold as a way to
help the financial and industrial sectors revive and attacked by many
as another example of business favoritism—Roosevelt quickly recognized the need to address mass social discontent and instituted
a vast relief and jobs program. Ironically, he had run for president
on a budget-balancing platform, a staple of conservative public
policy. But immediately after his inauguration, the president and
his Emergency Relief administrator, Harry Hopkins, implemented
a broad program of relief. Shortly thereafter, the Public Works Administration and its subsidiary, the Works Project Administration,
and later the National Youth Administration and a host of other
agencies organized work projects such as road and post-office construction and rural and forest cleanup, and provided (borrowed)
funds for local governments to build and repair schools, hospitals,
and recreational facilities such as playgrounds, swimming pools,
and community centers. At the end of the New Deal phase of
the Roosevelt years, in 1937–39, the Federal Housing Administration presided over the construction of thousands of units of
public rental housing, a program whose success incited the wrath
of powerful real-estate and banking interests.

The Federal Theatre, Art, Writers, and Music Projects employed thousands of writers, artists, actors, directors, and musicians
who had experienced the Depression as an unmitigated disaster.
These programs spurred some of the more creative artistic activity
of the twentieth century but were finally scuttled by an embattled
and weakened Roosevelt when, under the chairmanship of Texas
Democratic congressman Martin Dies, the House Un-American
Activities Committee launched a series of investigations of alleged
communist influence in these agencies. From 1938 to the beginning of the war, communist domination of the arts and education was a favorite topic of right-wing commentary and political
pressure.

With the end of the war in 1945, the same forces revived and expanded their allegations to include Roosevelt's successor, Harry S Truman, who never recovered from the assault. His first three years and his only full presidential term were preoccupied with defending his administration from the challenge that he was "soft" on communism. Presiding during the largest strike wave in U.S. history, involving virtually all the basic industries, Truman lost no time in condemning his strongest ally, the U.S. labor movement. When, after accusing Truman and the Democrats of coddling big labor and communists in government, the Republicans captured both houses of Congress in 1946, they lost no time throttling labor's power; Congress quickly enacted the Taft-Hartley amendments to the National Labor Relations Act, one of the cornerstones of New Deal reform. This was the boldest antidemocratic legislation since the nineteenth century when the Supreme Court in *Dred Scott* upheld slavery and defended segregation in the *Plessy* decision.

Despite the fierce attacks by conservatives and the Right against federal economic intervention and income supports, especially for the arts, these programs were modest by the standard of existing needs, and the New Deal remained committed in the first place to saving capitalism through a variety of programs in behalf of business. But it introduced two concepts that had previously been confined to wartime emergencies: the New Deal affirmed the role of the federal government in job creation; and its obligation to provide a floor under income by instituting jobless benefits, income support to the indigent, low-cost housing, and free health care and social services to the poor. Given that Roosevelt, like Hoover, was not about to draw blood from the stone of decimated business sectors, funds for these programs were raised by government borrowing at rates of interest that enriched financial institutions and had to be paid for, eventually, through raising taxes, primarily on income, but also on business. The conservatives criticized peacetime deficit financing of social programs precisely on these grounds, an ideological assault that prompted the so-called second New Deal to be framed within the contours of fiscal responsibility, the prime example being old-age pensions, or Social Security. As one of the leading architects of the program, Arthur J. Altmeyer, wrote almost thirty years later: "The President emphasized in his June 8 [1934] message to the Congress [announcing an executive order for the appointment of a committee to develop a social security plan] that he favored financing any long range program through a contributory social insurance system rather than by an increase to general taxation." Altmeyer was referring to several competing plans, especially to that proposed by a retired California doctor, "F. Townsend, which would allocate $200 a month for seniors over sixty years old, to be paid for by a 2 percent national sales tax. Townsend headed a mass movement that became a formidable force in his own state, providing a crucial impetus for the gubernatorial candidacy of Socialist Sinclair who ran as a Democrat, and lost, in that year's election."[11]

The social security plan was to include unemployment and workers' compensation, national health insurance as well as pensions. The pensions and the compensation programs survived the legislative process, largely because they were both contributory programs; the federal role was to administer rather than finance the programs out of general revenues. The health aspect of the plan fell by the wayside after four years of controversy during which the American Medical Association waged a powerful and ultimately successful campaign to sink any possible compulsory health program. In fact after years of study, the administration's bill, introduced by one of its most reliable legislative allies, New York's senator Robert F. Wagner, was significantly watered down and as he remarked at the time, "The bill will not impose . . . a straitjacket on state plans"—in other words, no compulsory federal program.[12] Weakened by the acknowledged opposition of the

AMA and the relative indifference of a rising labor movement, in 1939 the bill failed to become law and the goal of universal health care remains on the political agenda to this day. Perhaps Roosevelt knew that financing social insurance exclusively through the tax system would likely sink it, at least in the long run. In an era of conservative, business domination of the Congress and state legislatures, government-financed pensions and health care are once again subject to fierce debate. The current conservative offensive for privatizing every government service except the military and the space program must tread gingerly around the Social Security system, precisely because workers contribute more than 7 percent of their wages to pay for their benefit. While the self-interested insurance and drug companies may be the most potent forces arrayed against a universal, publicly financed health-care program, one cannot explain general business opposition in terms of self-interest alone. Employer opposition to government financing of a health plan attests to the power of ideology. Currently, in more than 80 percent of U.S. work places, employers contribute to employee health plans at a cost of 8–15 percent of payrolls and pay taxes for jobless benefits and workers compensation. Moreover, more than half of all U.S. workers have supplementary private pension plans through their work places, most of which are employee contributory but require substantial employer contributions as well. Yet, in spite of spiraling health-care costs, which have a significant impact on profits, and the cost to employers of supplementary pension programs, in an era of an aging workforce employer groups remain adamantly opposed to removing the cap on Social Security taxes in order to provide an adequate pension for U.S. workers, and are a leading force against a contributory health-care program—let alone a universal one—entirely funded by general taxes.

Even in the darkest days of the Great Depression when more than a quarter of the workforce seemed permanently unemployed and industrial production was relatively stagnant, leading U.S. manufacturers and corporate farms expanded overseas trade and investments. In 1934 U.S. armed forces fought rebels in Nicaragua, occupied Chinese seaports to keep the trade door of that country open, and protected corporate property at home against insurgent workers in San Francisco and in many southern textile towns during the national textile strike. Some of these skirmishes resulted in injuries and even the deaths of unarmed demonstrators, notably in the 1937 Chicago Little Steel Massacre, and in California, where migrant laborers challenged the growers, who stubbornly resisted their demands by summoning the National Guard and state police to break strikes.

Critics of the internationalization of U.S. capital trained their fire on two aspects of America's new corporate order: the breakneck pace of the formation of domestic monopolies and oligopolies that embraced nearly every major production industry and many retail sectors; and the formation of international cartels, especially between the U.S. steel, chemical, and electrical firms and their counterparts in Nazi Germany, such as Krupp and IG Farben. U.S. corporations like U.S. Steel and General Electric were accused by some of helping to finance the German war machine, while the independent capitalist Joseph Kennedy—John F. Kennedy's father—and several others enjoyed warm relations with high Nazi officials. At least for the half century between the Versailles treaty (1919) and the early 1970s, the United States emerged as the leading military, industrial, and political power in the world.

As in World War I, the United States prospered from World War II, consolidated its position as the leading economic and military power in the world, and with the development of nuclear weapons, had a temporary monopoly on this most lethal weapon of mass destruction, a possession that placed the United States at the helm of the "free-world" coalition. For the war's end did not result in disarmament. The Cold War, announced by Winston

Churchill in his momentous Fulton, Missouri, speech in 1946 and supported by the Truman administration, meant that the United States was committed to maintaining a large peacetime army and a spending program that constituted a veritable permanent war economy. By 1949, the Soviets, the other military superpower, had displayed their own atomic weapon, but the balance of nuclear terror that ensued did not deter either side from engaging in a furious arms race.

The terror balance inhibited either side from using nuclear arms, but the many wars in which the United States was and remains involved demand that a substantial portion of its public treasury be devoted to the production and maintenance of conventional arms and armed forces. While U.S. foreign policy after the war remains, in general, bipartisan, politics has divided on the fundamental question of whether placing the United States on a permanent war footing effectively forecloses fulfilling promises of domestic economic security such as guaranteed income, universal health care, and adequate publicly financed pensions. Given the growing distortion of the tax system, which has veered from its wartime-induced progressive character, the United States has, for better or worse, chosen to place resources in the private sector on the expectation that tax breaks for the rich will eventually translate into job-generating investment. As we shall see, the much-discussed emergence of globalization has thwarted even that expectation. Corporations have concentrated their loyalties among their own stakeholders, who demand handsome dividends. In pursuit of maximum profits, they have outsourced millions of jobs offshore and established corporate identities in foreign sites to evade paying taxes to the U.S. Treasury. In the process the national debt has grown to obscene proportions.

After World War II, only the Soviet Union challenged the United States, but mainly in two areas: military and scientific development. With U.S. assistance, the rest of Western Europe and

Japan spent the first two decades after the war in the arduous task of rebuilding their economies and political systems. The USSR had similar problems. Having lost more than twenty million of its citizens during the war and suffered substantial destruction of its industrial base and transportation and communications infrastructures, the regime was obliged, like its European neighbors, to shift considerable resources to reconstruction tasks. In addition, the Yalta and Tehran Agreements with the United States and Britain resulted in a bipolar world. Reversing its own concessions made to the victorious Germans at Brest-Litovsk—where as a price for peace, the Bolsheviks conceded a huge portion of the western border, principally Poland and Finland, but retained Ukraine, Byelorus, Latvia, Estonia, and Lithuania—the Soviet Union insisted on a wide swath of control over the territories it had conquered from the retreating Germans, including a portion of Germany itself.

These acquisitions proved, in the medium as well as the long term, to have been a mixed blessing. On the one hand, with grim memories of the war, which had been fought largely on Soviet soil until the final year, Stalin bargained for a large security zone between Western Europe and the Soviet border. He demanded, and won, control over Poland and the lion's share of the former Austro-Hungarian Empire, most of which had collaborated with the Nazis—the exception being Yugoslavia, where an indigenous, Communist-led guerilla army had pinned down several army divisions of both the Italians and the Germans in the wake of the Allied advance, from the east as well as the west. In return, Stalin abandoned to the British support of a powerful Communist-led guerilla force in Greece, much to the consternation of the partisans of that country. On the other hand, in the other countries, Soviet troops were obliged to field an occupying army that for ten years or more had to be fed, clothed, and housed. With the exception of East Germany and Czechoslovakia, these were mainly agricultural countries with sparse industrial development; Hungary and Poland stood somewhere in the middle, but the Poles were deprived of much of their industrial base by intense Allied wartime bombing. In all cases, the Soviets had to shoulder much of the burden of support for the local national military forces, even as the Red Army looted a large portion of their resources and brought the booty back to the Soviet Union. More ominously, the postwar arms race placed awesome burdens on the Soviet economy, its scientific and technological resources, and its capacity to meet the long-deferred demands of the people for the good life.

The United States bore its reconstruction burdens gladly. A decimated Europe sorely needed U.S. food and clothing and, more to the point, loans and gifts to rebuild its basic industries. Having received these through the Marshall Plan, Britain, Germany, France, and Italy placed large-scale orders to U.S. companies for aircraft, chemicals, communications and construction equipment, steel, aluminum, and other raw materials and, of course, cars and trucks. In the course of this mammoth rebuilding effort, U.S. corporations invested heavily in European and Japanese steel, auto, and electrical-equipment industries—in many cases establishing their own European and Japanese divisions—and built plants to manufacture cars and chemicals, but also purchased significant stock portfolios in European and Japanese firms.

By the late 1950s, Europe and Japan, while still oil dependent, were supplying their own needs for raw materials like coal, "capital" goods such as basic steel and other refined metals, and chemicals, and had reestablished their respective textile, clothing, and shoe industries. Gradually their agriculture sectors returned and achieved better than prewar production levels. France became the United States' chief competitor in global food markets. And European and Japanese car companies were producing for their own markets and, by the late 1960s, began to export their automotive products to developing countries and the United States.

It was not long before the U.S. economy began to feel the heat of global competition.

The last thirty years have been marked by a fundamental sea change in the economic, political, and cultural situation. By the mid-1960s, twenty years after the war, the economic reconstruction of Western Europe and Japan having been completed, the U.S. economy was severely challenged from abroad. Although partially masked by the Vietnam War–induced economic boom, even before its conclusion in 1975, Americans began to suffer the effects of recession and global competition. The 1969–70 recession was a harbinger of a new relationship of forces by which Western Europe and Japan posed a serious threat to U.S. domination of their internal markets, the U.S. market, and those in the less industrially developed regions.

From 1970 to the present, Japanese- and European-made cars, steel, and innumerable consumer goods flooded U.S. markets. This "invasion" in the midst of economic stagnation created, for a time, the revival of U.S. anti-Asian xenophobia, as the pundits freely predicted that the Japanese, whose cars were quickly increasing their share of the U.S. consumer market, were destined to overtake the United States as number one. Indeed, by the 1990s, Toyota and Honda had overtaken Ford and GM products in several categories as the largest-selling cars in the United States. But like its European counterparts, by the 1990s, the Japanese economy as a whole experienced a long-term recession. Still, the problem of why the United States had failed to maintain its once overwhelming lead in basic production industries needs to be addressed. We have already mentioned one factor: European and Japanese economic recovery made it likely that these countries would reclaim their own markets. But there is another factor. During the 1950s and 1960s, even as U.S. competitors were rebuilding their industrial base with the most advanced automation and cybernetic processes, U.S. corporations failed to invest in these advanced industrial technologies, and steel and auto provided the most serious examples. In fact, U.S. capital flowed into Japanese and German reconstruction efforts rather than into modernizing domestic industrial plants. It was not until the late 1980s through the 1990s that computer technologies and organizational changes such as "flexible specialization" were widely introduced into U.S. industrial plants. But in many ways these innovations were introduced too late to save large portions of the U.S. manufacturing sector. Even though wages were lower in key industrial sectors than those of Western Europe and Japan, U.S.-made products were outbid in many global markets because competitors had the technological edge and offered lower prices.[13]

In sum, while still powerful, the United States began to lose its undisputed economic hegemony and, with the formation of the European Union in 1977, its political dominance as well. During this period, battered by lower profit rates, leading U.S.-based corporations and their European and Japanese counterparts responded by transforming themselves into transnationals. This meant that much of the globe's industrial production in basic metals and chemicals and secondary sectors such as consumer goods manufacturing would no longer be concentrated in the main industrialized societies, especially the United States, which had, by far, been the world's most powerful consumer and producer of raw materials, machinery, and consumer goods. As the West Europeans and Japanese became major steel, auto, and machine-tool producers for global markets, in 1971 President Richard Nixon abrogated the Bretton Woods agreements that stabilized the world's currencies around the U.S. dollar, and the dollar began to "float" against the yen and leading western European currencies. Nixon was attempting to protect U.S. exports because a relatively devalued dollar would lead to cheapened U.S. products that could successfully compete abroad. The strategy failed to halt the long-term slide in the balance of trade. One of the enduring themes of the 1970s and 1980s and of the current century is the deficit in global trade.

Another symptom of the decline of U.S. economic dominance was the so-called productivity crisis of the 1960s and early 1970s. This was an era of significantly slimmer profit margins in many important economic sectors. American workers drove up the price of their labor both in higher wages and improved health and pension benefits, and as Martin Sklar and James O'Connor argued at the time, the revolt against work itself in auto and other major industrial plants led to stagnant productivity. Strikes, job actions, sabotage, lateness, absenteeism, and simple malingering, especially by young workers, paralleled the far more dramatic and politically sophisticated struggles against the alliance of the state with capital in many European centers, especially in France and Italy in 1968 and 1969. That these events did not lead to a fundamental reappraisal of power relations led to a ferocious and prolonged counterattack by capital, the end of which is still not in sight. Once viewed by many, including professional economists, as dead and buried, neoliberal economic doctrine came roaring back.[14]

According to this doctrine, all possible forms of state regulation were conceived as distortions of the free market; protective tariffs should be removed; and labor, just like any other commodity, should compete with itself, now on a global scale. Among the most important consequences of this doctrine is the rejection of advances in the welfare state and proposals for its gradual or rapid dismantling, the pace of which was entirely dependent upon political resistance by the underlying population, particularly seniors, the black freedom movement, and the labor movement. Deregulation became the order of the day, and none was more compliant than the U.S. Congress, which in the late 1970s—under a Democratic administration—revoked banking and transportation rules, reduced farm subsidies, and, after the enactment of Medicare in the 1960s, all but froze the main elements of the pension, health-care, and income-support systems. Seen in this context, the so-called Reagan Revolution was prepared by a decade of bipartisan retreat from many New Deal regulatory innovations.

TWO

THE REAGAN REVOLUTION, THE CLINTON "BOOM," AND THE DOWNSIZING OF AMERICA

What Was the Reagan Revolution?

N O ACCOUNT of the development of twentieth-century U.S. economic, political, and cultural development can ignore the significance of the eight years of the Reagan presidency. Recall that Ronald Reagan's predecessor, Jimmy Carter, had failed in his attempt to lead his fellow Americans in a moment of national self-reflection, when, in the wake of the onset of a global economic and political crisis, the fate of the nation had not been as uncertain since the Depression. Reagan strode into his second term of office on the heels of the unresolved Iran hostage crisis. His administration rapidly negotiated the hostages' freedom and proceeded to revamp many of the traditional expectations Americans had harbored about the role of their government since the New Deal. Declaring that the era of "big government was over," in its first year in office the Reagan administration secured the passage by Congress of a huge tax cut, mostly for upper-income individuals and corporations; announced an imminent reform and privatization of the Social Security system to give corporate insurers a chance to bid for the business; and, in August 1981, fired eleven thousand striking air-traffic controllers—their union had supported Reagan's election—for violating the federal no-strike law. The AFL-CIO, at least in numerical terms still formidable, slumped to the occasion rather than calling for massive protests, and its callow response—begging Reagan for amnesty—opened an era of concessionary bargaining. Many unions gave up hard-won work rules, especially those protecting their members from outsourcing; agreed to wage freezes and even reductions; and signed long-term no-strike contracts.

In the end, however, Reagan lacked the political will to carry his privatization program to its most controversial conclusion: privatization of Social Security. As we have seen, unlike antipoverty programs in which the beneficiaries had been constructed as malingerers, the Social Security system was contributory, and the millions of contributors had a strong sense of ownership. Reagan's reforms were suspected of being dismantlement, and the accusers were not entirely wrong. As the president hesitated at the precipice, in 1983, David Stockman, the budget director, resigned and accused the administration of backtracking on its bold conservative course. Reagan proved to be a superb practical politician with Teflon skin. His administration sent a battalion of marines to Lebanon to clean the country of guerilla fighters who were harassing Israel. When they returned with huge casualties but no victory, Reagan suffered no appreciable political liabilities, largely because the Democrats were still in the thrall of foreign policy bipartisanship. He was soundly defeated during the nationally televised 1984 presidential debate with Walter Mondale, his Democratic opponent, but suffered few negative consequences. Instead Reagan

seemed to evoke sympathy from an electorate that remained sus-
picious of smart people, anyway. And in the late 1980s, amazingly,
his administration illegally transferred to Nicaraguan contras funds
obtained from officially sanctioned secret drug traffic to fight the
Sandinista regime, a scandal about which Reagan protested he had
no knowledge. The American people and their congressional representatives were forgiving; the president was not impeached but
retired from office as a legendary symbol of American hope.

The Reagan "revolution" was as much cultural as economic
and political. Americans were advised to expect less from government, except, of course, its duty to defend the country against what
the president termed "the evil empire." Reagan introduced the
doctrine, faithfully followed by George W. Bush, that the state was
constituted as a global police force and an adjunct to big business.
It was a startling series of declarations for, even if these were, in fact,
the chief state functions throughout America's nineteenth- and
twentieth-century history, no president since William McKinley
had used his bully pulpit to openly acknowledge this fact. On
this doctrine, even as he articulated the ideology of small government and fiscal restraint, the Reagan administration strong-armed
Congress to pass the largest peacetime military budget in U.S. history. After Reagan's resounding reelection victory, with the help
of Democratic senator Bill Bradley of New Jersey, in 1986 the administration crafted a second tax cut, the size of which remained
unmatched until George W. Bush put his own signature on two
cuts within his first term, emulating the regressive character of Reagan's reverse Robin Hood legislation. Fearing voter retribution,
the Democratic-controlled Congress obediently passed the bill.

The first two years of the Reagan White House were reces-
sionary; official unemployment reached double digits as investment soured. But tax cuts and especially military Keynesianism
proved good enough medicine to create a five-year bubble until,
during George H. W. Bush's term, the new president was forced to

deal with the consequences of Reagan's hubris. When, to prevent a meltdown of the treasury, he raised taxes, Bush lost part of his conservative electoral base to billionaire Ross Perot and went down to defeat in the 1992 presidential election. But the profound shift in political and economic discourse had been effectively planted. Neoliberal economics became the new state religion. If any politician of ambition and stature questioned the sanctity of the free market and the need for cost containment in government as much as in private enterprise, his goose was likely to be cooked.

Under the sign of "cost containment," a euphemism for job destruction and wage reductions, in the mid-1980s, capital embarked on two decades of relentless displacement of living labor by finally introducing many technological innovations into the U.S. workplace—not only by automation and computerization of large chunks of the labor process, but also by changes in organization such as "flexible specialization" or just-in-time production, the dimensions of which we will explore in Chapter Four. Needless to say, manual labor has not disappeared, but it has lost much of its centrality in the U.S. economy. By the 1980s, the good-paying union factory job that included benefits and an array of rights that protected the worker from arbitrary discharge and unwarranted discipline had become as rare as a vintage bottle of expensive wine. The intensification of labor was amplified by employer demands for compulsory overtime, for relaxation of hard-won work rules that ameliorated the vicissitudes of industrial discipline, and for employee contributions to union-negotiated health and pensions plans. Exemplified by well-known labor struggles of the period—such as the 1985 Austin, Minnesota, Hormel; the Decatur, Illinois, Caterpillar; and other Midwest strikes—where workers resisted these demands and lost, once powerful unions felt obliged to grant concessions to employers in the hope that by restraining wage and conceding work protections, their jobs would become more secure. It proved to be a one-sided deal.

For even as the 1980s and 1990s have been heralded as an era of relative prosperity, this was a period that witnessed the loss of more than nine million production jobs, and the first three years of the new century have seen nearly three million more disappear. The rise of countries such as Mexico, China, and India as major centers of industrial production and intellectual and technical competence is due, in no small measure, to the flight of transnational capital from the United States, and the labor movement has been unable to slow, let alone halt, the flow of jobs to these regions. While liberal commentators such economist Robert Reich assured us that there was nothing to worry about because the displaced worker will rejoice in her new status as a "symbolic analyst" in the new, gleaming hi-tech economy—and the rise of the dot.coms seemed to confirm his confidence—the new century ushered in a period of dot.com bust that lingers in the midst of a so-called economic recovery.

Contrary to neoliberal and classical expectations, we have entered an era where the structural link between investment and jobs seems to be broken. Official unemployment rates hover around 6 percent despite a rise in the Gross Domestic Product, and the statistic, which is based on the number of people actively seeking work, has been constrained by millions of discouraged or pushed-out workers between eighteen and sixty-five who have left the labor force and are no longer counted as unemployed. This has been a jobless recovery, where the new work that has been created is temporary, contingent, part-time, often poorly paid, and lacking benefits.

And the retail sector remains phlegmatic largely because during this recovery, which should have produced higher prices and wage increases, prices and wages have been flat. Unlike the '80s and '90s when retail and hi-tech jobs took up some of the slack of lowered manufacturing employment, neither sector is prospering. In fact, workers in the relatively well-unionized retail food-chain industry are hard-pressed to hold on to their standards when Wal-Mart, a virulent antiunion giant competitor, pays close to minimum wages, offers almost no benefits, and imprisons night employees by locking them in the workplace. In October 2003, nearly seventy-five thousand grocery-chain workers struck against four California-based grocery chains, a strike that was still in process in the beginning of the new year. The main issue of the strike was the demand by employers that workers agree to sharp wage and benefit reductions to enable them to compete with nonunion Wal-Mart. It has become abundantly clear that what may be defined as a "living wage" of seventeen dollars an hour has, from the perspective of many employers, proven prohibitive, in retail trades as well as in large portions of goods production. The strike was finally settled when negotiators agreed on substantial union concessions; at the same time, the employers failed to substantially abrogate the benefits programs, one of their major objectives.

"The Downsizing of America"

The world has turned 180 degrees since 1984, when, borrowing a trope from Bob Dylan, Ronald Reagan boldly declared it was "morning in America." The Reagan "revolution," which still is the political coin of national policy and drives the public conversation, has been a roller coaster of boom and bust, global bravado and global military adventure, and periodic revelations of corruption in high and intermediate places of power. Neither the "downsizing of America"—a term of the 1990s that began in the 1970s with "deindustrialization"—nor the alarming exodus of jobs abroad has abated the economists' persistent claims that free trade and deregulation are good for our economy. The central argument was, and remains, that global production reduces labor costs, and consumers benefit by the resulting lower prices and the reduced threat of inflation. Quoting such diverse sources as Clinton's secretary of labor, the liberal Robert Reich, and conservative Gregory Mankiw, President Bush's chair of the Council of Economic Advisors, *New York Times* reporter Eduardo Porter assures his readers that although jobs are "hemorrhaging," job creation is just around the corner. (The theme is repeated on the paper's op-ed page by Columbia economist Jagdish Bhagwati, who assures us that technological change rather than outsourcing is the major cause of job loss, and as in the past, we are on the brink of a new burst of high-paying jobs: In the end Americans' "increasing dependence on an ever-widening array of technology will create a flood of high-paying jobs requiring hands-on technicians, not disembodied voices from the other side of the world."[1]

Despite these soothing words, skepticism is rampant in a land where millions of workers at every level of the occupational structure are without solid prospects. If politics is defined by different and competing visions and programs for social rule, it is also a time when the idea of politics itself is under a cloud. Rancor and anxiety about creeping unemployment may spread in the ranks, but consensus prevails at the commanding heights of economic and political power. Although Democrats dispute Republican initiatives and, in Europe, Socialists decry the growing influence of the Far Right, in practice, the religion of free trade, the imperatives of military Keynesianism, and cost containment in entitlement programs spans the political spectrum. If the Bush administration hesitates as Alan Greenspan suggests that severe cuts be made in Social Security and Medicare, its circumspection may be attributed to political expediency rather than to conviction. Yet when a liberal politician or a labor leader dares to express doubt, we can be sure that, from the *New York Times* to the *Wall Street Journal*, from CNN to NBC, the news media will come down like a ton of bricks on suggestions of caution about, let alone opposition to, free-trade policy. Or on the ground that he is not a viable contender because of his slim treasury, the media chooses to ignore 2004 presidential candidate Dennis Kucinich's proposal during the primary season that trade agreements such as NAFTA and the World Trade Organization be repealed. Legitimate opinion, it seems, depends on the size of your wallet.

In the past quarter century, we have absorbed new terms to describe the underlying conditions that confront Americans, among which "deindustrialization," "globalization," "wage stagnation," "consumer confidence, "outsourcing," and "productivity" occupy pride of place. Most people who came of age in these years have grown accustomed to job and income insecurity and uncertain personal prospects and have learned not to trust politics and politicians. Perhaps more to the point, young people—and many of their elders—believe that government or elected officials have little to offer in their quest for a modicum of well-being, and many have declined to participate in any form of politics, even voting. For those for whom politics still matter, at least to shape their economic prospects and financial security, the farthest horizon is to hope that, like physicians, government will first do no harm.

Since Nixon's Watergate and Reagan's own contribution to the long tradition of official misfeasance and disinformation, the Iran/contra affair, we have learned not to expect candor from our political leaders. The rhetoric of politics is subterfuge, half-truths, and even outright lies. The last public White House acknowledgment that the unparalleled U.S. prosperity of the post–World War II era was coming to an end was President Carter's declaration, in cadences of teeth-grinding moral introspection, of a moment of national reflection about the dark times ahead. Carter's angst earned him virtually universal scorn and, together with the Iran hostage crisis, may have cost him reelection. Despite their anxiety, or maybe because of it, Americans do not like to hear bad news and are likely to blame the messenger rather than explore deeper causes of national malaise.

In a country awash in double-digit inflation and the slow but steady exodus of relatively well-paying manufacturing jobs to the nonunion South, both of the United States and the Mexican border, Reagan came to power exuding unbounded optimism—a stance Americans, despite mounting evidence to the contrary, were all too willing to entertain. The strategic outlines of the newly installed administration were embodied in an extensive 1981 report, *Mandate for Leadership*, issued by a leading conservative think tank, the Heritage Foundation. In more than a thousand pages that covered thirty-two policy areas, ranging from agriculture, defense, health and human services, and commerce to scientific policy, the arts, and all the major regulatory areas, conservative experts offered their plans for the new administration.[2] The main ideological outlines were these:

1. On the premise that the Soviet Union's military procurement program was far more extensive than that of the United States, dramatically increasing defense spending and reducing trade with the Soviet bloc and China;

2. Declaring that competition and economic growth are inhibited by unreasonable federal controls over commerce, significantly reducing regulations;

3. To further the objective of ending big government, transfering many federal responsibilities to the states;

4. To free the market from unfair federal competition with business, privatizing public goods as fast as possible and getting the government out of the business of running programs by outsourcing their administration to private companies;

5. Freeing the intelligence "community" from administrative burdens and promoting laws and administrative polices that permit more clandestine collection of information, without heavy burdens of congressional oversight.

During the Nixon presidency, the Democrats had remained defensively committed to a whittled-down version of New Deal domestic programs. Ratified by the Bretton Woods Agreement, which installed the U.S. dollar as the fulcrum around which all currencies revolved, the dollar was, for almost three decades after World War II, the staple currency of global markets. But in the wake of Nixon's abrogation of Bretton Woods in 1971—a tacit recognition that the United States was no longer able, unilaterally, to dictate the terms of international trade and investment—and the introduction of the long winter of economic stagnation after the mid-1970s, the Democrats retreated on a broad front. The Carter presidency was the first self-proclaimed neoliberal Democratic administration. Senator Ted Kennedy, the accepted paragon of social liberal hope (a euphemism for a version of New Deal regulation and welfare), sponsored trucking deregulation, and the liberal House Banking Committee chair, Henry Reuss, introduced legislation to deregulate most banking transactions. It was Carter, not a Republican president, who signed these bills. The results were disastrous for smaller truckers and wrecked havoc in labor relations in this industry. Banking deregulation led to an avalanche of mergers and acquisitions, as well as an invasion of large banking corporations into local markets, and resulted in the demise of many locally owned savings-and-loan associations and independent banks. Anticipating the Heritage report's intelligence proposals, Carter oversaw the establishment of a secret court to sanction surveillance by intelligence agencies of organizations and individuals suspected of subverting national security, a measure that foreshadowed the Bush administration's Patriot Act. And it was Jimmy Carter's misfortune to preside over the steepest inflationary spiral since 1951, a product of the new reality of globalized trade, especially in oil and other energy resources, and the free-falling dollar, a consequence of the cancellation of Breton Woods and the declining fortunes of America's international economic position.

With both political parties firmly committed to free markets, deregulation, and smaller government—mostly as semi-religious belief rather than practical policy—the political opposition is relegated to the margins; its options are limited to protest and resistance, except for the odd congressional maverick like Dennis Kucinich (an endangered species) and freewheeling populist dissenters such as Ralph Nader and Pat Buchanan, who have no effective legislative or electoral expression. To utter ideas such as federal protection for depressed industries and products on the one hand, and economic equality and economic security through the expansion of public goods on the other, is to invite derision at best and accusations of disloyalty at worst. Despite rancorous partisanship, which usually takes the form of invective arising from financial and personal scandals like embezzlement and adultery, most of which are worthy merely of a daytime soap opera, actual differences between the major parties are, except at election time, miniscule.

Driven by their belief that the public discourse has become irreversibly conservative, in the late 1980s under Bill Clinton's leadership, Democrats, whose centrists regrouped under the banner of the Democratic Leadership Council, claimed the territory of constraint and caution. In a historic reversal, Republican administrations from Reagan to the Bushes opt for spending sprees (mostly on the military) and huge tax cuts for corporations and wealthy individuals that produce moatlike fiscal shortfalls. Long identified with smaller government (a euphemism for cutting social spending, especially in time of war), the GOP has abandoned fiscal conservatism and now favors deficit financing to fund its aspiration to world leadership—without, however, wearing the label of military Keynesianism or restraining its appetite for producing technologically awesome weapons and undertaking expensive space travel. While the Democrats have hesitated to follow Republican demands for privatizing Social Security and Medicare, school vouchers, and other rightist domestic policies, they have embraced the core of neoliberal policy doctrine: cost containment, balanced budgets, and free trade.

The Reagan program of open war on public social spending was not unveiled in a vacuum. In the first place, it presupposed deindustrialization and economic stagnation. It was prepared as well by the New York City fiscal crisis of 1975–76 during which, under pressure from international currency markets, banks, and other financial institutions, banks staged a veritable capital strike against what they regarded as profligate public spending on 1960s social and economic programs for the working and unemployed poor. Of course, the response of the Democratic city and state administrations was characteristic of contemporary liberals: They surrendered well before the battle was actually waged and, in the name of austerity, proceeded to slash education, health, and income programs for the poor. In 1977, the Carter administration and its senatorial ally, the liberal Ted Kennedy, began the process of ending business regulation. The 1978 California referendum approved Proposition 13, which limited the ability of government to raise taxes by legislative action, followed by a series of parallel measures in many states, especially Massachusetts. While remembered as a remarkable instance of grassroots power, the initiative actually had the financial and political backing of business and conservative elites. Forgotten is the 1979 $400 million in wage concessions granted by United Auto Workers members to the Chrysler Corporation as the price for securing an infusion of government funds to keep the company in business. This huge giveback ushered in a new concept, which reigns in current labor relations: Workers can make no gains unless they grant productivity and other concessions to employers—in which case the gains are, in fact, losses.

During his first year in office, Reagan sent two powerful signals that he intended a decisive break with the past, even with the conservative policies of the Eisenhower and Nixon administrations.

Riding a wave of tax revolt, the president persuaded a groggy, divided Congress to pass a huge tax cut that mostly benefited corporations and wealthy individuals and immediately plunged the federal treasury into red ink from which it did not recover for seventeen years; and as we saw, Reagan fired eleven thousand striking air-traffic controllers for violating federal antistrike law. In contrast, Nixon had responded to the 1970 unauthorized strike by postal workers, except for a few highly visible retributive acts against a handful of alleged strike leaders, by ordering the National Guard to move the mail, which proved to be an exercise in futility. After a shaky start, owing largely to a two-year recession, Reagan hit on his third major innovation, intended, in part, to address the sagging economy. Reagan submitted to Congress a record peacetime arms budget, which was sold as a deterrent to the alleged expansionist plans of the Soviet Union, now dubbed "the evil empire." In the process, we saw the emergence of the Reagan doctrine that went beyond the historic U.S. foreign policy of containment. Now U.S. policy reached for the objective of destroying the Soviet empire and subordinating the Chinese. Congress complied, and, aided by huge infusions of fictitious capital into the economy in the form of generous government contracts, the rest of the Reagan presidency resembled prosperity (fictitious capital is money that rests on credit—funds that are spent before they exist in real terms). The administration pursued a health and social-welfare policy strongly advocated by *Mandate for Leadership*: "HHS [Health and Human Services] must foster legislation and an administration that fully implements a competitive approach to health care delivery. Its posture ought to be put in terms of minimizing its role as a government entity, reducing its regulation, opposing legislation that would expand its role, and instead devising statutes that would enable and at least enhance the private sector's innovative approaches."[3] The report goes on to advocate "regulations" that would "starve out public interest law firms" and, in the interest of encouraging private initiative, deregulate government oversight of day-care centers and other social services.

Reagan did not hesitate to cut funds for people who needed income assistance, and he drastically reduced many social programs, including federal aid to education and public health. Reagan's budget director, David Stockman, vigorously pursued legislation that would substantially privatize Social Security and Medicare, a proposal Republicans revived again and again in subsequent years. However, consistent with his performance as California governor, Reagan was not anxious to incur the ire of the growing legions of senior citizens who viewed these proposals with alarm. Retaining his rhetoric of free-market competition, the president backed off from Stockman's Social Security privatization plan. In disgust and disappointment, Stockman, a true believer, resigned and wrote a book that condemned Reagan for betraying true conservative principles. But Reagan was not a consistent fiscal conservative. Stockman should have looked at the military budget for a clear indication of Reagan's agenda. He would have discovered a fervent advocate of huge government expenditures to help stimulate the sluggish economy and to bankrupt the Soviet Union, the principal global adversary of the United States. Both aspects of the strategy proved to be brilliantly successful. Faced with a deep slump that was not entirely of his own doing, Reagan used the tools of government economic intervention that had guided his predecessors: While forcefully refusing the route of job creation in social goods and enhanced income support for the unemployed, he pursued the Truman-Eisenhower-Johnson program of military Keynesianism using the same Cold War justification: thwarting the Soviets.

Cold-warrior political commentators praise the Reagan administration for its forceful pursuit of military spending in order to bankrupt an already weakened Soviet regime. But the arms race was not a sufficient condition for the collapse of the Soviet Union. The regime buckled under the weight of bureaucratic and authoritarian rot but also faced other more immediate obstacles to its survival. The arms race did limit the capacity of an otherwise weak and declining regime to provide a richer selection of badly needed consumer goods, and forced significant deterioration of its once pioneering health and pension systems. But the regime's main problem was that it could not raise capital. With oil prices falling, the Soviets lost an edge bestowed by their best export commodity. At the same time, having encouraged the reformers of the Gorbachev government, under the slogans of glasnost, to liberalize its political control—Gorbachev finally dismantled the gulag and made political dissent more legitimate within the country— Reagan and Bush Senior brazenly abrogated their promise to grant an $11 billion loan to help stabilize the regime. With few capital resources to modernize the consumer-goods sector and upgrade the seriously impaired welfare state, and saddled with a corrupt and incompetent state bureaucracy and an industrial managerial class that was eager to inherit the still considerable fixed-capital resources under its command, the effect of Reagan's arms policies was only to accelerate what had been all but inevitable since the twenty-year stagnant and dilapidated Brezhnev regime.

Runaway prices, the bane of the economic existence of workers and retirees on fixed incomes, had marked much of Carter's term in office. Since the late 1980s, consumer prices have remained relatively stable, except for housing and health-care costs, which together tend to drain the incomes of average Americans. In the last thirty years, there has been virtually no real growth in the national economy, if by "growth" we denote expansion of real economic resources such as the production of basic commodities— capital goods (machinery and raw materials) and durable consumer goods, chiefly single-family homes, appliances, and cars. In my use of the term "real," I refer to the actual quantity of goods and services that derive from domestic capital investment, including wages paid to U.S. workers, and exclude "spurious" or fictitious capital that is raised through the accumulation of public debt that is a result of the permanent war economy. I contend that it is precisely the gap between profits and real domestic capital accumulation that accounts, in its broadest compass, for the high level of unemployment and underemployment in the U.S. economy since the late 1970s.

Faced with economic stagnation in real terms, U.S. capitalism has attempted to recoup sagging profits by means of "financialization." In the past two decades, financialization has taken America by storm. The term refers to the tendency of the contemporary U.S. economy to focus on money transactions, rather than industrial production. Investments boom in mergers and acquisitions of insurance companies with banks (for example, Citibank and Travelers), of two or more giant communications corporations such as those that comprise today's Verizon, Time-Warner (which includes the Internet provider AOL), ABC-Disney, and many others. People take out second and third mortgages on their homes to finance their children's schooling, frequently switching credit cards to obtain lower interest rates or to have funds available to speculate in the stock market. None of these transactions or "investments" creates a net increase in jobs or material wealth. In fact, many of the mergers and acquisitions of the 1990s destroyed jobs: The merged corporations did not require duplicate services like two bank branches across the street from each other, or staff for two parallel of Internet providers. Mergers were an intrinsic component of the decade of downsizing, a decade that, except for its last two years, experienced wage stagnation and decline when money wages were discounted for inflation. As Randy Martin has pointed out, for many, financialization became a way of everyday life.[4] Since nearly 50 percent of all Americans have some stake in the stock and bond markets, many of us spend part of our free time handicapping the daily trends and use the Internet to shift money from one stock to another or, if we are invested in mutual funds, from stocks to bonds, and back again. We find ourselves constantly shopping for lower credit-card rates to transfer our debt, an activity that can take several hours every week, and for this purpose accumulate credit cards rather than savings. These activities are conducted for private protection and gain and have loosened our collective appetite for improving public goods.

Unemployment, in both real and official terms, reached double-digit levels during the Reagan recession of 1981–83 and, except for the last three years of the Clinton presidency when it declined to about 4 percent, remains today well above the postwar average. Millions of women have entered the paid labor force, so that household income has not dropped even as individual wages continue to erode or stagnate. Many women work part-time, mostly in retail trades, where wages hover around the legal minimums, or in food services such as restaurants, supermarkets, and catering establishments. For the past four years, nearly ten million workers are officially jobless at any time and, in despair, millions more have quit looking for paid work and for this reason are not counted in the statistics. A recent report issued by the progressive National Jobs for All Coalition estimates that if involuntary part-time work and discouraged workers are added to the 5.6 percent official jobless rate of early 2004, the actual rate is 11.7 percent, nearly identical to most countries of Western Europe. While European countries calculate the involuntary part-time and discouraged workforce in their statistics, the U.S. government standard does not. One of the most significant features of federal employment standards is to count anybody who has paid work as employed and not to count discouraged workers who are no longer looking for work as part of the labor force. This accounts for the disparity between the workplace and the household surveys. U.S. labor statistics are constructed to hide the extent of joblessness.[5]

In fact, it was during Reagan's two-term presidency that the pervasive phenomenon of "deindustrialization" exploded to the surface of public conversation. In June 1980, *Business Week* issued a warning that America's competitive edge was eroding under the weight of large-scale plant closings. Two years later, Barry Bluestone and Bennett Harrison provided grim detail of what had become a common practice among some leading U.S. industrial corporations. U.S. Steel announced a layoff of thirteen thousand workers and the closure of fourteen mills; in the 1970s, General Electric "expanded its worldwide payroll by 5000, but it did so by adding 30,000 foreign jobs and reducing its U.S. employment by 25,000." And RCA, Ford, and General Motors indicated they had all but abandoned expansion of their domestic production facilities but were planning major expansion overseas. The authors concluded that growth had all but ceased in the U.S national economy, in part because its key engine, industrial production, had stalled. They calculated that throughout the 1970s, the United States had lost thirty-eight million jobs due to private disinvestment, especially of plants and equipment.[6] At the same time, service jobs blossomed, especially in health care and retail, but most were poorly paid relative to factory jobs. By the 1980s, women had become the main breadwinners in many households.

During the watch of Reagan's successor, George H. W. Bush, the economy stumbled badly under the weight of the aftershock of the 1987 stock-market crash and the mounting balance-of-trade deficit caused, in part, by a decade of deindustrialization. By 1990, Wall Street banking and brokerage firms had "downsized" by 20 percent. New York financial services, which employed some 350,000 workers before the crash, employed 280,000 in 1990. In the doldrums of recession, the last two years of Bush's presidency were marked by a resumption of offshore capital flight by corporations, not only of intermediate-technology industries such as textiles and clothing, but now in advanced-technology sectors such as information giants IBM, Eastman Kodak, and Xerox. Upstate New York communities, the mid–Hudson Valley, and Rochester were left in a state of shock, especially at IBM and Kodak, where employees had resisted union organization for two generations largely on the strength of corporate no-layoff policies. The 1990s raised the specter that outsourcing would increasingly mean exporting jobs abroad rather than to the traditional destinations—rural southeastern states.[7]

The Clinton "Boom"

After our auto caught fire and burned in the late 1990s, it was time to buy another used car for our summer residence in upstate New York. We saw an ad in the local newspaper for a 1988 Chevrolet Cavalier, and the description and the price were right. When we arrived at the owner's residence, a mobile home park in a town about twenty miles away, we discovered that he was a "retired" IBM employee. After we bought the car, we sat down for a cup of coffee and some talk. It turned out that he had worked as a technician and had been promoted to a low-level administrator at the company's recently shuttered Saugerties, New York, plant. Like many of his fellow employees, he was not offered a position in another location, nor was he qualified to collect a full pension. He was more than fifty-five years old but had worked for the company just short of the length-of-service requirement. He was able to find another much lower-paying job but was forced to sell his house and use the proceeds to buy a mobile home. Many employees in similar circumstances had accepted without protest the company's buyout offer, but he joined with a minority of them to sue the company for violating the agreement upon which many employees had been hired: no layoffs regardless of economic conditions. I never got word about the outcome of the case, but I assume the company settled out of court with their disgruntled former employees rather than expose itself to a long, public trial.

Despite frequent announcements of job shedding by large corporations, the impact of this news in our national conversation was somewhat mitigated by the fact that the 1990s were a watershed decade for what became known as the information "revolution." Remember, this was the "new economy," when on nearly every Sunday-morning talk show, one could find Bill Clinton's secretary of labor, Robert Reich, exalting in the arrival of a new era that would produce a raft of "symbolic analysts" to replace many of the good manufacturing jobs that continued to go away. So enamored was much of U.S. public opinion with the shining high-tech future that awaited us that we engaged in collective "forgetting" of past assurances by politicians, economists, and pundits that the era of the business cycle in which prosperity was inevitably followed by recession was over. Never long on memory, we forgot how during the 1950s writers like Adolph Berle and David Lilienthal declared an epoch of "people's capitalism," signifying that by means of mass stock ownership most Americans would eventually become stakeholders in the capitalist system, abolish poverty and unemployment, and enjoy progressively higher living standards. Equally important, Reich predicted the new economy would end the cycle of boom and bust that had marked the globalization of industrial production. If people's capitalism means that many Americans own a small cache of stocks and bonds, we have reached it. But if people's capitalism means that we rely on these investments to take care of our retirement income, they are much less secure than the Social Security system. In fact, during the two slides of the past fifteen years—1989–93 and 2001–3—millions of Americans watched their personal safety nets disintegrate as the financial-services sector, especially the stock market, swallowed up a hefty chunk of their life savings. Yet we cling to the image of the golden 1990s.[8]

Indeed, even many skeptics at first were almost persuaded, for the rapid expansion of the home-computer market exceeded even the wildest dreams of the leading manufacturers. From 1994 to 2000, annual personal computer (PC) and printer sales rose by an average of 20 percent, which meant that production and sales more than doubled in a little more than half a decade. For a time, it appeared that the proliferation of new companies in the software section of the industry and the consequent demand for trained technicians to service millions of newly acquired home computers had created a skilled labor shortage whose end was nowhere in sight. The last half of the 1990s was a seller's labor market as much as a seller's goods market in computers. Although computers had long been a staple of the industrial, white-collar, and service workplace and the Internet was already a fixture in upper-middle-class and professional homes, the spread of PCs and the Internet—in addition to providing access for millions to the global marketplace as much as information—allowed individuals and groups the rush of instant communication through e-mail and conferencing.

Schools at all levels of the academic hierarchy scrambled to buy computers and establish degree and nondegree programs— from computer science, computer programming, and engineering to word processing and basic operation. Colleges reported severe teacher shortages in technical and scientific fields; not only were salaries uncompetitive with those offered by a burgeoning private sector, but the schools were not turning out enough qualified labor either in teaching or in management and information services (MIS)—the department that maintains and repairs the software and the networking features of institutional communications. Since in colleges and universities, the administration usually supplied a computer to every faculty member and departmental administrative staff, with a fairly generous cache of equipment for students as well (often at the expense of hiring new professors or teachers), the information services departments matched the computer science and technical departments in growth and commanded an increasing percentage of the institutions' budgets. Salaries in these departments rose rapidly and, in time, were often substantially higher than those of humanities and the social sciences. But the new information technology did not stop at computer-based communications. Beepers were already in wide use by the late 1970s. Handheld wireless telephones, a relative novelty until the late 1980s, became a vital device for a whole layer of business professionals from truck drivers to stock traders and swiftly extended for social use to private individuals.

At first, IBM, Kodak, and dozens of blue-chip companies, which had prospered in the halcyon decades of war and Cold War economic environments, disdained an aggressive entrance into some areas of consumer electronics. Possessing a virtual monopoly on mainframe computers, IBM was slow to adapt to the introduction of the home-based personal computer and consequently permitted Japanese and U.S. hardware and software companies to acquire a dominant segment of the market. By the time the Big Blue cast the scales from its eyes and began to produce PCs, Japanese corporations like Compaq and Toshiba, joined by U.S.-based hardware producers such as Hewlett Packard (HP) and Gateway, the custom assembler, had captured a huge segment of the market; and HP became dominant in printers, although Japanese producers such as Canon, Epson, Brother, and others claimed considerable market shares. The invasion of Fuji in the U.S camera business and the failure of Kodak to move swiftly in research and development of digital cameras imperiled the company's overwhelming power in the camera and film markets. While, belatedly, IBM introduced the Thinkpad in the laptop sector of the home computer industry, the company was forced to spend huge sums and years in the game of catch-up. In the early 1990s, it closed several plants and laid off more than forty thousand employees, and finally joined many other information corporations in outsourcing some manufacturing.

Kodak was even more derelict; having lost ground, it began the slow hemorrhage of its main Rochester, New York, facility by abolishing some fifteen thousand jobs in the late 1970s. Throughout the 1980s and 1990s, local residents and workers became accustomed to a slow but steady stream of job losses, but in 2004, the company declared its intention to move many jobs overseas. To accomplish this task, Kodak announced a massive layoff of another fifteen thousand, seven thousand in its home city. When completed, Kodak's disinvestment in the city will have reduced its Rochester workforce from seventy thousand in the late 1960s to about thirteen thousand, a loss of about 80 percent.

As dramatic is General Electric's massive exodus from Schenectady, New York. Once the flagship plant with twenty-seven thousand employees of this largest of all U.S. industrial corporations, in 2004 there were only two thousand left. And the company seems to have an aversion for cities, having closed several New Jersey plants and its Cleveland facility in favor of bucolic, nonunion rural settings. Needless to say, in recent years, GE has gone global. And General Motors and other auto corporations are not far behind. According to a *New York Times* survey: "Whereas the General Motors Corporation employed 500,000 people at its peak in the 1970s, twenty years later it can make just as many cars with 315,000 workers. Computer programs rather than lawyers prepare divorce papers."[9] In the new century, GM's production workforce has been further reduced.

The Best Republican President of the Twentieth Century

In 1996, the *New York Times* published its special report *The Downsizing of America*, based on a series of articles published earlier in the newspaper. The report chronicled the growing awareness that "millions of Americans are losing good jobs." Among its findings, the *Times* calculated that forty-three million jobs had been "eliminated" between 1979 and 1995. "Many of the jobs would disappear in any age, when a store closes or an old product like the typewriter yields to a new one like the computer. What distinguished this age are three phenomena: white collar workers are big victims; large corporations now account for many of the layoffs; and a large percentage of the jobs are lost to 'outsourcing'—contracting work to another company, usually in the United States." To be sure, add the authors, "far more jobs are being added than lost. But many of the new jobs are in small companies that offer scant benefits and less pay and many are part-time positions with no benefits at all."[10]

It may be argued that job loss was basically associated with the Reagan–Bush Senior era and that, as Paul Krugman insists, Clinton reversed many of its worst features. Between 1994 and 2000, the economy added about three million jobs a year. Although tens of thousands of skilled and semi-skilled jobs were created in the dot.com boom, many of them were not "jobs" in the conventional sense of the term because they did not provide benefits such as company-paid health care and supplementary pensions. Many computer people worked as contract laborers. Moreover, in the wake of the sudden 2000–2001 "bust" that witnessed the bankruptcy or merger of hundreds of "start-up" software companies and even the merger of some established hardware firms, notably Compaq's absorption by HP, the disappearance of many of the recently created jobs left thousands stranded. At the turn of the twenty-first century, long-term, relatively well-paid jobs carrying benefits are the exception rather than the rule in the information industries. And even those whose jobs are not immediately threatened feel insecure as they read about leading corporations shedding thousands of jobs, many of which are the result of outsourcing of skilled technical and professional work to China, India, and other overseas countries, and others due to a well-known feature of late-capitalist societies—overproduction in relation to the capacity of the market to absorb products. In 2000–2, capital investment in information industries dropped sharply and stocks in the technology-rich NASDAQ lost 60 percent of their market value from its high point in March 2001.

These losses cannot be blamed entirely on Clinton's successors. They resulted from cyclical overproduction of hardware and software in relation to a depressed global market. But even at Microsoft, half the workers did not have health care, stock options, and other benefits because they were hired as "contractors" and were paid slightly more to purchase their own insurances. On the wager that they would reap "new-economy" riches, thousands of computer scientists and technologists shrugged off benefit packages as they joined budding dot.com enterprises. When the boom imploded, many aspiring millionaires who had quit their more secure employment to throw in with the start-ups were left in the lurch. Unless they were hired on as contractors or consultants (which saved the employer up to 25 percent in benefits alone), their best short-term chance of income was state jobless benefits. For this was a period when finding a job in computer-mediated fields often took a year to eighteen months.

The Clinton administration agreed with the information industry that commercial transactions on e-mail should be free of taxation and, perhaps more importantly, became a major promoter of start-ups and openly courted the newly flush hardware and software entrepreneurs on the West Coast, from Silicon Valley to Seattle; and Vice President Al Gore joined Robert Reich in attempting to assuage the discontent and disillusionment of union members and their families who were experiencing the pain of job losses. Preferring to rely on quiet diplomacy by the administration's adroit ambassador, former vice president Walter Mondale, Clinton spurned pleas from the leadership of the Steelworkers union for some tariff protection against what it viewed as illegal and unfair "dumping" by the Japanese. Nor, as the volume of Japanese- and Korean-made automobiles surged in U.S. markets—they eventually reached nearly a quarter of all cars sold—was he more sympathetic to the brazen protectionist "Buy American" campaign of the United Auto Workers, a slogan which conveniently ignored the reality that, even as they retained domestic assembly operations, the leading companies outsourced the production of many auto parts abroad. As he entered office, Clinton was not yet a full-throated free trader; indeed, during the 1992 campaign, he had expressed serious doubts about unfettered trade agreements. After waffling on the measure for most of his first year in the Oval Office, the president signed the North American Free Trade Agreement in 1993, which included some labor and environmental protections. Armed with his vision of a high-tech future for the U.S. economy, and staunchly claiming that removing barriers to the movement of capital, goods, and labor across the borders of Canada and Mexico would be good for U.S. workers, Clinton became one of the more reliable free-trade presidents of the postwar era. And when the administration's deeply flawed universal-health-care measure failed to pass a divided Congress the same year, his favorite slogan, "It's the economy, stupid," became the administration's major concern.

By his second term, Bill Clinton was America's leading trade representative, and corporate America had no more competent advocate. But the president's program for expanding trade was directed not primarily to finding ways to facilitate the export of U.S.- made goods, but to making the global climate more favorable for U.S. investment, especially in Latin America and Asia. Clinton's close confidant Commerce Secretary Ron Brown traveled the globe seeking outlets for U.S. capital that could not find domestic outlets. Among the "favored" nations for U.S. investment, none stood higher than China, Canada, and Mexico. The terms of agreement were that the United States would impose few, if any, barriers to goods made in these countries, and, in return, they would welcome U.S. capital without imposing tax burdens or onerous labor laws on corporate investment. In addition, the World Bank and International Monetary Fund would advance loans to these governments to build plants and the material infrastructure systems needed for producing and moving goods: roads, dock facilities, and electricity. With the able assistance of the Clinton administration and global financial institutions, the 1990s was a period when countless U.S. corporations—the big-three auto companies and electrical and appliance producers—outsourced billions of dollars and tens of thousands of jobs to the so-called maquiladoras along the border near El Paso, Texas, and Juarez, Mexico. Less visible was a parallel migration of U.S. capital to Canada. But the big fish was China with its billion and a quarter population and a government powerfully intent on modernizing the country through industrialization.

In the first half of the 1990s, attracted by proximity to Fudan University—China's equivalent to MIT—Dupont financed a huge petrochemical complex in the Poudong area near Shanghai, using Chinese intellectual as well as manual labor. The Chinese government reciprocated by supplying the infrastructural conditions. The area near Hong Kong became a major production center as well, and throughout China, Thailand, and the Philippines, U.S.-based manufacturers of apparel systematically transferred the bulk of their operations. Even the relatively automated U.S. textile industry was not far behind. Believing that it was protected from domestic disinvestment by high-tech machinery and work processes, by 2000, the exodus of mostly southern textile mills to China and other sites in Southeast Asia was in full force. Indeed, despite frequent disputes between the Chinese and the administration, the Clinton years made indelible contributions to the trend in U.S. foreign policy begun by Richard Nixon when he made his historic China trip in 1973. In the shadow of the Vietnam War, U.S. capital, supported by the government, has vastly expanded its interests abroad and—despite the importance of U.S. military interventions in Bosnia, Afghanistan, and Iraq—not chiefly by military means. Nor, despite the significance of Middle Eastern and Venezuelan oil, is U.S. policy mainly directed to securing raw materials. Raw-materials acquisition is by no means abolished from capital's global concerns. But what is new about U.S. foreign policy since Clinton is its preoccupation with addressing the chronic limitations of the domestic market for capital and commodities. Consequently, at all levels, U.S.-based capital is today invested in industrial production and electronically based services on a global scale and, as we have seen, has ruthlessly subjected U.S. plants and services to the criterion of cost effectiveness. Absent a new technology, which at best can engender a short-term burst of jobs and sales, the frontier for investment remains offshore. The main legacy of the Clinton years is to have elevated this strategy to an undisputed principle. With the assistance of the U.S.-controlled World Bank and International Monetary Fund, multilateral and bilateral agreements are, by means of loans and grants, sharply focused on prying open markets for U.S. capital.

Spurred by huge personal-debt accumulation, the 1990s witnessed a boom in retail sales. Many manufacturing jobs were replaced by Mcjobs—those paying at or slightly above the minimum wage—a term that honors the leading retail-restaurant chain.

During the boom, the Clinton administration rode its wave and claimed some of the credit. But the Clinton administration, like all others, heralded the phenomenon of job creation as such and never acknowledged that a job paying as much as nine dollars an hour was in many regions of the country below the poverty level. And at McDonald's, Burger King, and Wendy's, wages for counter clerks were closer to six dollars and short-order cooks were paid only slightly higher wages.

After the Democrats lost both houses of Congress in the midterm election of 1994—some observers attribute their House loss to Clinton's attempt to thwart Richard Gephardt's presidential ambitions, a favor to Al Gore, and to the inept management of the administration's health care plan, which would have delivered huge profits to managed-care and drug companies but at the same time would have raised taxes to pay for benefits—Clinton's economic program relied on a second hallowed principle of conservative policy: fiscal austerity. As the economy recovered from four years of doldrums—largely due to a heavy infusion of new capital into the information industries, the retail sector, and the merger-and-acquisitions movements, which enriched shareholders and jump-started the most sustained stock-market bubble in memory—Federal Reserve chair Alan Greenspan began a steady drumbeat that warned the administration and the public of the dangers of inflation. Greenspan is a follower of the arch-right-wing philosopher Ayn Rand and a longtime devotee of one of the major architects of free-market ideology and small, public goods–free government, Milton Friedman. As soon as the economy began to recover, he opened a focused campaign to convince leading members of the administration that to prevent inflation, a balanced budget based on restraint of social spending had become a vital imperative. At the same time, he urged employers, private and public, to resist workers' demands for substantial wage increases.

Using his powers of persuasion but also the Federal Reserve's control over interest rates, Greenspan adopted a policy of what he termed the "traumatized worker." He deployed the threat and the practice of raising the prime-interest rate to slow demand, especially for consumer durables such as housing, and to discourage wage increases, which would heat up the economy too much. Employers took Greenspan's cue and, despite the alleged economic surge, stubbornly resisted union wage demands. As a result, in a time of prosperity for some, the Clinton era was marked by an unprecedented decline in real wages. To add insult to injury, during his second term, Clinton reappointed Greenspan, who had been heralded in business circles as a "genius" for stemming inflation by throttling labor.

The Clinton administration and most congressional Democrats became ardent converts to the doctrine of smaller government. Under Vice President Al Gore's direction, the Clinton administration proceeded to cut about four hundred thousand federal jobs, mainly through attrition; held the line on military spending; and eliminated or reduced the size of hundreds of social programs. Declaring that the "era of big government is over," facing reelection in 1996 Clinton signed the newly installed Republican Congress's major first-term objective, which even the ever-popular Ronald Reagan was unable to achieve: in Clinton's words, "the end of welfare as we know it." Under the so-called Welfare Reform Act, which went into effect in 1997, millions who received income support from the federal government were informed that their benefits would end in five years; those capable were required to participate in work programs as a condition of qualifying for their checks. The work assignments were usually for twenty hours and, together with their welfare checks, paid the prevailing minimum wage and provided no subsidies or programs for child care. State governments swiftly established welfare-to-work programs, which usually consisted of cleaning streets, public buildings, and parks; hospital maintenance and patient care work; and other tasks. Despite the legal requirement to provide training and education, these services were generally not provided; in some states, like New York and California, the welfare clients replaced unionized workers earning nine or ten dollars an hour. Nor did state governments provide funds for child care for clients who were obliged to work. In New York State, welfare clients who had enrolled in the two large public universities were not able to claim their course work as a work assignment, an injustice eventually partly remedied, but this privilege was extended to clients in few other states. When workfare participants attempted to organize in order to present their grievances over onerous working conditions, in many states they were refused a hearing and were threatened with removal from the rolls if they persisted. Since there were no enforceable federal labor standards to protect clients forced to go from welfare to work, except for the provision of the minimum wage, they were left to the mercy of the states, few of which filled the vacuum.

The Clinton years confirmed and reinforced the fundamental doctrines of the Reagan Revolution: the abrogation of the policy of government as employer or income provider of last resort. Clinton tacitly accepted the prevailing conservative view of the unemployed poor as people who needed a metaphorical cattle prod to arouse them from the grip of the "culture of poverty," according to which they had become habituated to not working. At the same time, the Welfare Reform Act was exhibit A of the concept of "tough love" that had become the centerpiece of conservative social-welfare policy. As with the Johnson administration's War on Poverty thirty years earlier, the notion of structural unemployment—according to which there were good reasons to assume the existence of a chronic job shortage—was strictly excluded from policy considerations. Instead, on the assumption that in a dynamic market economy, unemployment was a "frictional" or temporary condition, the poor were themselves responsible, if not entirely to blame, for their own joblessness.

In this process we can observe the convergence of both major political parties on incomes and other welfare policies. The Clinton administration, no less than the Bush regime, denied the elementary insight of John Maynard Keynes expressed in the dark days of the Great Depression—that the relation of profits, wages, production, and consumption tend to equilibrium, but at a level below full employment. From this proposition, Keynes derived the necessity for government economic intervention to insure that "effective demand" for capital and for commodities was maintained. Among the measures to be taken, income support through job creation and outright grants for the unemployed were by no means primary, but these occupied an important place in his recovery program. After initial resistance to the relief programs of Presidents Hoover and Roosevelt, the conservatives reluctantly reconciled themselves to providing food to the indigent to alleviate starvation. And, of course, it was Hoover, not Roosevelt, who initiated the establishment of government institutions to provide low-interest loans to stimulate business investment. But a benchmark of conservatives' confidence in the market was expressed in unrelenting opposition to Roosevelt's work programs. Under the WPA and related agencies, millions of workers were employed in building roads and cleaning forests and streams, in a variety of arts programs, and in the development of huge electrification projects such as the Tennessee Valley Authority (TVA) and the Grand Cooley Dam. By the time of Johnson's War on Poverty, these highly visible activities to rebuild America's physical and cultural infrastructure had lost pride of place and were replaced by short-term stipends to the poor who enrolled in education and training programs or were employed in the public-service sector.

While after World War II the main political parties agreed on a bipartisan Cold War foreign policy, they reserved their differences largely to domestic issues. Since the hegemony of Clinton's Democratic Leadership Council, we have seen bipartisanship on all essential issues. Clinton substituted workfare for education and training and shunned the expansion of public goods that could accompany job creation for a policy of shrinking the government. Whereas, in the name of helping the poor, Johnson and the Democratic Congress appropriated billions of federal dollars to assist states to create jobs in education, health, and social services and thereby expand services, under Clinton the states and the local communities were left to fend for themselves. Nor did Clinton do more

than any of his predecessors to advocate a "peace dividend"—
substantial federal expenditures for schools, health care, and other
public goods. In fact, at best his administration engaged in a policy
of benign neglect, and at worst he became a relentless privatizer
by promoting outsourcing of federal functions to private corporations.

After surviving a series of personal scandals during which he
was impeached by the House of Representatives, Clinton left office basking in the sun of economic success. While official joblessness remained at its lowest point since the early 1970s, the Clinton
legacy was deeply implicated in giving new meaning to what a later
politician called the two Americas. In contrast to the earlier "other
America" pronounced by Michael Harrington in his famous 1962
book, this time the two Americas did not signify the divide between
the rich and middle class on the one side and a large minority of
poor people on the other.[11] When a candidate for the Democratic
presidential nomination, North Carolina Senator John Edwards,
decried the "two Americas," he referred to the "disappearance"
of the consumer middle class, a hybrid of well-paid unionized industrial and service workers, professional and technical employees,
and small business owners. It was not only the poor who were on
the other side of the divide; many in the so-called middle class
for whom the American dream had become something of a reality until the 1970s had become downwardly mobile. Although
Edwards's polemic was directed to George W. Bush's three years
of economic woes for this social layer, it is important to remember that critics had already noted the trend toward oligarchy and
plutocracy since the mid-1980s. Even as Reagan had blithely ignored labor's urgent pleas for government action to slow, let alone
halt, capital flight, while not oblivious, Clinton offered the "new
economy" as a salve to the disconsolate. His genius consisted in
a remarkable ability to retain support among those most battered
by the globalization of the U.S. economy. He felt their pain.

THREE

IT'S THE TECHNOLOGY, STUPID

I F THE CLINTON years were marked by fiscal austerity, W's administration may prove to be the most profligate in modern history. In his first term, Bush led the United States into two wars, which became the rationale for a sharp increase in military spending. The president also revived Reagan's discredited defense-shield proposal (popularly known as Star Wars) and declared that in the future, America would spend billions to send a spacecraft to Mars. Then, on the eve of his reelection campaign, Bush sent to Congress a $400 billion Medicare-reform bill that would a provide prescription-drug benefit to retirees, largely by transferring public money to drug companies. Within weeks of its passage, Medicare's chief actuary announced that the program's cost had been seriously understated by $152 billion, or 40 percent, an allegation that almost got the official fired for spilling the beans.

There are two standard neoliberal solutions to recession: At the monetary level, reduce interest rates in order to stimulate business investment; and fiscally, cut taxes in order to expand consumer demand and business spending. Following this playbook, since the recession that began in March 2001, the Federal Reserve Bank reduced the prime rate to 1 percent, a near vanishing point, and despite frequent announcements during 2003 and the first quarter of 2004 of spectacular quarterly growth, Federal Reserve chair Alan Greenspan steadfastly refused to raise interest rates to stem inflation. Of course, there was a question of whether there even was any real inflationary trend. But when oil prices skyrocketed in the spring and, despite a dip in housing construction, home prices soared in anticipation of an interest-rate rise, talk of raising the prime rate spread throughout global equity markets. Greenspan finally relented in June 2004 by raising interest rates by a modest .25 percent.

With congressional approbation, the Bush administration sharply cut taxes in two large chunks that total $1.25 trillion, distributing the benefits unevenly to large corporations and the wealthiest 2 percent of the population on the argument that the wealthy and the corporations are likely to spend and invest more, and jobs would be created. For the others, Bush awarded every tax-payer either a $350 or $600 lump-sum payment, and some upper-middle-income families reporting more than $100,000 could gain about $5,000 in their 2003 returns. Taken together with the military-spending spree and the Medicare giveaway, the administration increased the national debt by almost $2.5 trillion. By 2004, the debt stood at $7 trillion. Not unexpectedly, ever the loyal supplicant to the Right, Greenspan, whose passion for fiscal austerity is confined to Democratic administrations, remained silent and did not warn of the dire consequences of an unbalanced budget and bloated debt, such as the danger of runaway inflation. Baffled, like most neoliberal economists, Greenspan continued to express concern that somehow the measures taken were not producing jobs, even as in some sectors, particularly financial services such as banking, profits recovered handsomely.

Meanwhile the balance of payments and trade deficits kept skyrocketing because the price of the dollar on international exchanges plummeted in relation to the Euro, the yen, and other currencies, and Americans continued to purchase foreign goods in mounting and distressing volume. The dollar's fall reflected sagging domestic industrial production, which expresses itself in the 2.7 million jobs decline since March 2001 and a rising balance-of-trade deficit that hit record proportions in early 2004. Foreign investment in U.S. Treasury bills and other means to pay the accumulated federal debt declined because of the plunging interest rate. In fact, without Chinese investments in U.S. currency, given rising oil and other commodity prices, Americans might have found themselves in a whirlwind of galloping inflation. As the country entered the election season, the stock market reacted to these trends with extreme volatility, careening from peaks to valleys but generally sliding from its late 2003 highs. The pundits, always prone to contingent explanations, found many reasons to account for the plunge in the first quarter of 2004—the terrorist attack on a Spanish commuter train, anxiety as the Pakistani army searched for the Al Queda's second-in-command, the anemic monthly jobs reports—and stocks rose on the Federal Reserve's refusal to raise interest rates in the wake of rising industrial production. Search the business pages and the reader finds little in the way of political/economic explanation. According to prevailing expert opinion, profit rises should—but don't—lead to overall recovery.

Paul Krugman continues to blame the economic malaise on the Bush administration's wanton disregard for prudent fiscal policy. The AFL-CIO targets corporate offshore outsourcing and calls for some protection against the most job-destroying aspects of the prevailing free-trade policies. In the primary races of fall and winter 2003–4, the eventual Democratic presidential candidate, John Kerry, proclaimed his loyalty to free trade but endorsed some outsourcing constraint and pointed to the ballooning debt, a theme echoed by some Republican fiscal conservatives. But Kerry and the conservatives part ways on whether to rescind the huge tax breaks for the wealthy; taking a leaf from the 1980s tax revolt, the conservatives want to reign in spending but, of course, would exempt the military. In late March, Kerry proposed a reduction of two percentage points in corporate taxes but would refuse tax benefits to companies that shipped jobs overseas. Some Republican legislators called for taking a second look at the huge bill for funding the Medicare reform. Which leaves health, education, veterans' benefits, and the environment to bear the brunt of any new austerity program, an unlikely eventuality in a closely divided electorate, especially among seniors, who have the bad habit of going the polls.

Typical of the Right's reading of the current economic situation is that of Christopher Caldwell, senior editor of Rupert Murdoch and William Kristol's ostensibly neoconservative *Weekly Standard*. Writing in the *Financial Times*, Caldwell recalls Bill Clinton's famous campaign motto, "It's the economy, stupid," to warn John Kerry and the Democrats that they should not be too optimistic about the outcome of the 2004 presidential election: "The president's fiscal policy—an expensive war, thousands of billions of dollars in tax cuts—may fly in the face of the economics his constituents learned in university. But the economy has grown snappily for eight quarters. Whatever long term financial liabilities the Bush administration has saddled the country with, these are unlikely to be reflected in immediate voter misery on Election Day."[1] Caldwell relies on the "bottom line" of rising corporate profits, media reports of robust recovery, and the media's capacity to argue that the economy is in good shape.

But the glaring omission in Caldwell's optimistic tale is jobs. And this account could be repeated throughout the Right's unflinching support for the thesis that the U.S. economy is indeed on the upswing. What conservatives fail to ask is whose ox is gored by growth without substantial new job creation or rising wages. For example, even as the GDP rose by 4 percent in the fourth quarter of 2003, wages increased by a weak two-tenths of 1 percent. As we have previously noted, official unemployment rates were constant during the so-called recovery, not only because job creation failed to outpace job destruction but also because, after months of futile job searches, millions of discouraged workers have left the labor force, which indicates that the labor force is shrinking. How would the optimists deal with a 2004 *New York Times* report showing that nearly half the black men in New York City are without jobs? Or the huge losses of well-paying factory jobs in the past three years sustained by Michigan, Ohio, and other industrial-heartland states? Why hasn't the usual shibboleth that trade leads to jobs come true? Or where is the commentary about the failure of the huge bump in military spending to produce hundreds of thousands of new jobs?[2]

It is impossible to devise a program that addresses chronic joblessness unless we assess its actual extent and are able to analyze its underlying causes. In the main, the tendency of conservative and liberal economists alike has been to rely on contingent, conspiratorial, or ethical explanations for the paradox. Or they rely on the conventional wisdom that economic growth invariably leads to job growth and we simply must be patient. Trapped in their own assumptions, the Democratic economists and policy analysts tend to blame the Bush administration's fiscal recklessness, its pro-business trade policies, and the costs of Bush's militarism—a reference to the wider foreign-policy debate. Accordingly, if a Democrat occupied the White House, jobs would reappear because the new president would adopt more prudent fiscal policies and reverse the Bush administration's preemptive unilateralism, thus cutting the costs of our military involvements. Academic and business economists, associated generally with the conservative interpretation of neoliberal economics, are either baffled by the disparity between growth and chronic joblessness or hasten to assure us that a healthy rate of job creation is just around the corner.

Job Growth Is Just Around the Corner

Before we take a closer look, we need to clear up two misconceptions: what the extent of joblessness actually is, and what we mean by economic growth. For if the jobless rate is actually only 5–6 percent, while it remains too high, it is scarcely of crisis magnitude. And if real growth in the domestic economy rises, there might be reason to believe that even the most relentless cost cutting will reach its limits and job growth will inevitably follow. The problem is that official statistics are woefully inadequate.

Here are the data for the year 2002 when involuntary part-time workers and non–job seekers who want a job are counted:

> Officially unemployed workers: 8.4 million
> Involuntary part-time workers: 4.2 million
> Non–job seekers who want a job: 4.7 million
>
> Total: 17.3 million

A true estimate of joblessness would subtract the aggregate part-time wages from the average full-time wage during 2002 of about fourteen dollars an hour. If this method of calculation were used, the U.S unemployment rate approximates that of most western European countries, 10–12 percent. And to obtain a more nuanced picture, demographic differences need to be factored in. For example, the official jobless rate for all blacks in 2001 was 8.5 percent. When the missing workers are added, the percentage leaps to 13.5 percent. In 2001, the number of discouraged workers was about equal between men and women. By the year 2003, men outnumbered women in the missing labor force by more than two to one, reflecting, it seems, the heavy loss of factory jobs compared to losses in the retail and other sectors of services.

But if we consider that 16.4 million full-time year-round workers in 2002 earned less than the poverty level of $18,104 for a family of four, the extent of underemployment is much greater in the United States than in western Europe, where poverty has been more substantially reduced. Add the 2.2 million adults languishing in U.S. prisons and we might arrive at a real unemployment rate that exceeds 15 percent. (In 2004, the poverty level is closer to $20,000, and as everyone knows, except the official statistics, even in rural areas and the Deep South no household can live on official poverty-level income. According to a United Way survey, for example, in 2002 the minimum comfort income for a Queens, New York, household of four was $43,000.)[3]

Writing in the *New Yorker*, James Surowiecki has advanced another explanation for the persistence of relatively modest unemployment data:

> Statistical expediency and fiscal obfuscation have become the hallmarks of this White House. In the past three years, the Bush administration has the Bureau of Labor Statistics stop reporting mass layoffs. It shortened the traditional span of budget projections from ten years to five, which allowed it to hide the long term costs of tax cuts. It commissioned a report on the aging of baby boomers, then quashed it because it projected deficits as far as the eye could see. . . . A recent report from the White House's Council of Economic Advisers included an unaccountably optimistic job-growth forecast, evidently guided by the Administration's desire to claim that it will have created jobs.[4]

Surowiecki bemoans the administration's apparent break with a long tradition of bipartisan executive-branch honesty in reporting economic data. In his view, the problem is the decline of the authority of the federal government's civil-service professionals and the politicization of information.

Previously, I have mentioned that much of America's economic growth data is based on fictitious capital. I define the concept as capital that rests on debt, whether private debt or government spending that exceeds revenues. An example of fictitious capital: Millions of Americans have gone into debt to purchase houses and fill them with furniture and appliances, to buy new cars, and to send their kids to college. Except for homes and cars, which usually require a relatively small down payment of 10–15 percent, most of the other stuff, including student loans, is bought on pure credit—which means that, at the time of purchase, purchasers have little or no equity in the commodity. Similarly if we take a trip, the flight's cost is usually put on a credit card rather than paid for in cash. Or the government spends hundreds of billions that exceed current revenues. The fictitious capital results in more economic activity: Money is invested, some jobs are created, but the money to pay for raw materials, machinery, and wages has no underlying basis, even though the credit company, usually a bank, advances the payment to the retailer, who in turn pays the distributor or manufacturer. Credit is a promise to pay in the future for today's purchases. Most debtors are able to pay in full for the goods or services we buy. But increasingly, even if fully employed and certainly if laid off, many cannot meet the monthly payments and must default. In the year 2003, more than a million Americans declared bankruptcy because they simply were unable to pay their bills. In these instances, banks sell the home or car for slightly more or less than the unpaid portion of their mortgage, transactions that are counted as services. In short, the definition of "goods and services" includes not only manufactured goods, but also the vast network of wholesale and retail transactions. To be sure, the balance-of-payments and balance-of-trade deficits—which seem to be as chronic as joblessness—are deducted from the Gross Domestic Product, but if a company invests its capital overseas but assembles part of it in the United States, the whole investment is considered "domestic."

The End of U.S. Technological Supremacy

In 1974 I published a short book, *Food, Shelter, and the American Dream*, on the current food and energy crisis. During my research I made what for me was an amazing discovery: After Europe recovered in the 1950s from wartime devastation, the United States no longer retained its near monopoly over the production of capital goods such as steel and other metal products; Japan and Western Europe were already supplying their own transportation-equipment needs—cars, trucks, and rail stock and cars; televisions, radios, and computers were produced for export by Japan and Germany; and many countries had resumed the production of textile products. In all these cases, other countries were producing both for their own markets and for markets that were once dominated by the United States. Recognizing these changes, U.S.-based corporations began investing in foreign companies. General Motors, Ford, and Chrysler all established British and German subsidiaries to compete with local car corporations and succeeded in driving most of the British car industry out of business. By the 1970s, Europe and Japan were exporting steel, electronic equipment, and autos to the United States.[5]

The upshot of my "discovery" was that, from the global perspective, even though only 5 percent of the workforce is engaged in agricultural activities of all kinds, America's genuine economic niche is as the premier global agricultural and energy producer and, until the 1990s, the world's leading knowledge producer. Since the industrializing era of U.S. capitalism when farming and other farm-related activities such as food and cotton processing and the production and distribution of farm machinery occupied 80 percent of the labor force, agriculture has remained a crucial element of the productive capacity of the economy. In contrast to Europe, where land scarcity, cultural traditions, and low levels of investment restricted productivity and kept food prices high, the productivity of U.S. agriculture made possible the production and distribution of vast quantities of cheap food, which helped to hold down wages and increase capital accumulation. The huge advantage of U.S. agriculture was created by plentiful fertile land, by the most technologically advanced machine and chemical industries in the world, and by a culture that willingly accepted the technological fix for economic troubles. In this respect, technology signifies capital-intensive methods of production: extensive use of machines in the planting, sowing, and processing of food but also the extensive employment of scientifically based methods of plant and animal breeding, use of chemical fertilizers, and, since the 1990s, of genetically modified organisms to enhance productivity.

In the 1990s, China and India abolished the U.S. monopoly over technological expertise in agriculture, textiles, and knowledge industries, and the U.S. government's refusal to ban or even label genetically modified organisms from its food exports has dramatically reduced what remains this country's most powerful trade commodity. For since the 1940s, the United States has exported almost 40 percent of its annual agricultural product. And when the mad-cow scare emerged at the end of 2003, Japan, which is among the best customers for U.S.-grown food, declared a beef embargo until the Bush administration vastly improved its inspection system—a step which, at this writing, it had yet to fulfill.

Battered by global competition, by the late 1960s, U.S. growth rates had slumped from their sixty-year average of 3 percent a year to 2 percent and, in some years, even less. As we have seen, productivity rates—a function of output per labor hour and of wage/price ratios—were sinking below growth. Richard Nixon's abrogation of Bretton Woods signaled that the old models were obsolete. The size of the U.S. economy, the strength of the unions, and sharp competition from emerging players such as Japan and Germany combined to constrain America's prospects for expansion. And, having decided that importing crude oil was cheaper than performing domestic drilling, America's insatiable thirst for gasoline was threatened by foreign oil producers who insisted, fatefully, on their economic, if not their political, autonomy. These were the multiple determinations that conspired to radically alter how America does business.

Since the 1970s, U.S.-based transnational corporations have systematically pursued a post-Fordist strategy, "post" because it departs from the conventional twentieth-century regime of industrial production characterized by highly centralized, vertically integrated plants that brought together thousands, sometimes tens of thousands, of skilled and unskilled workers, and is indifferent to whether domestic wages and salaries increase to purchase mass-produced goods. This strategy has four main elements:

- Dismantling as much of the U.S.-based industrial structure as is necessary to maintain profit rates, especially the power of labor to control wages and production standards;
- Outsourcing parts production both within the United States and to developing countries;
- Heavily investing in labor-destroying technological innovations and its concomitant: replacing, as much as possible, manual with scientific and technical labor, and

eliminating the traditional functions of middle management, which, after all, is an overhead cost that has negative
impact on productivity;
- And, as we saw in Chapter Two, reorganizing the workplace by, among other innovations, eliminating large inventories and warehousing by introducing "just-in-time"
production, or flexible specialization.

These strategies are directed in their effects, as much as possible, to
reduce labor costs by on the one hand putting labor in competition
with itself and on the other eliminating labor.

"Technology" became the driving force of the U.S. economy. By technology, I signify the introduction of not only labor-
saving machinery, but also forms of business organization such
as horizontal (that is, global) production and flexible specialization. But the fundamental transformation is that scientifically based
knowledge—especially the science of cybernetics, with its feed-
back, digital controls, and the introduction of chips that can store
vast quantities of knowledge/information, and that can be dis-
seminated to a wide variety of applications—controls the production of things as well as information that is largely "immaterial."
In this process, the worker is still a vital component of the labor process, but in many cases, not primarily as a direct producer.
The machine—computer or automated console—seems to regulate the production process, and in many sectors of the economy,
the worker has been assigned to different functions: to develop
the program that guides the machine, monitor the apparently
self-managed machine, and perform repairs. Taking the product
to the shipping room, packing it in containers or barrels, bring-
ing it to the loading dock, and loading it on trucks or railcars
have become semi-automated steps in the labor process. In addition, the worker keeps records by inputting information onto the
computer.

In the old *vertically integrated* industrial structure pioneered by the Ford Motor Company and emulated by many others, a single plant or, more commonly, a complex of geographically proximate plants produced everything except the primary raw materials—coal and metals ore. At its River Rouge plant near Detroit, Ford once employed as many as 120,000 workers and at least 60,000 between World War II and the 1960s, when, instead of modernizing the plants, Ford began to decentralize most of its operations. These workers operated a steel mill, a foundry, rolling mills, a wire mill, and a stamping plant and delivered internally produced finished parts to the assembly line, which was located nearby. Today, there are less than 10,000 people working at River Rouge. The meaning of the term "outsourcing" may be understood as the antithesis of vertically integrated production. Now Ford and other car corporations engage in *horizontal* production. Vertical integration has yielded to deterritorialization and decentralization, even as control is still concentrated at the top of the organization. While in earlier years, GM's and Ford's production facilities were heavily concentrated in Detroit and secondarily in Cleveland, Chicago, Saint Louis, and other Midwest cities, many of the newer plants are located in towns in border states and the U.S. South. They are unionized but lack the political traditions of auto workers in the Detroit area. Moreover, since the local economies are predominantly rural and permanently depressed, they have become virtual company towns. Any threat of capital flight sends tremors throughout the region. In most instances, GM and Ford operate their own assembly plants but outsource parts production. According to the new regime, if the machine is still assembled near consumer markets, the United States is still the heavyweight of global consumer society. But these corporations have established plants in Mexico, Brazil, and China to meet local demand as well as ship cars back to the United States. While retaining many plants within the U.S borders remains politically as well as economically necessary, parts may be manufactured anywhere and by any small or large company. The typical auto-assembly plant draws almost all the parts used in the car from external sites, both within the United States and offshore.

For decades, nearly all these parts plants were under union contract and observed union standards. But in recent years, this arrangement has become too costly for car companies, which, despite their global reach, have lost nearly 25 percent of their domestic market share and since the late 1970s have given ground to European and Japanese firms in almost every national market around the world. Backs to the wall, in some cases the United Auto Workers has negotiated concessionary contracts that, in addition to establishing two-tier wage systems in some plants and despite strong contract protections, tacitly permit management to outsource parts production; in others cases, the companies have violated existing agreements by engaging in sub-subcontracting.

Decades earlier, similar concessions were granted by the needle trades unions. To preserve their benefits funds and their more skilled crafts, the unions agreed to permit manufacturers to contract to nonunion shops, as long as they maintained their welfare-fund payments and a small cutting and pattern-making facility. But the old Ladies' Garment Workers Union (now part of UNITE, Union of Needletrades, Industrial, and Textile Employees) even tolerated substandard wages and working conditions in union shops. In New York's Chinatown, for example, community organizations and investigative reporters discovered union shops that paid below minimum wages and sanctioned long hours and even child labor. Of course, decentralization has been made possible by high-speed air, ship, and train transportation, as well as by the differential labor costs between the unionized Northeast and Midwest and the mainly nonunion U.S. South, and between advanced capitalist countries and developing societies such as China and Mexico. In short, "Made in the U.S.A." is both literally and metaphorically a shell of the truth.

It was not too long ago that Americans were being reassured that the end of the era of the "rust belt" of intermediate-technology industries such as steel and textiles, although painful, would be a short-lived transition to the development of a "new economy." Many industrial jobs might disappear, but most would be replaced by professional and technical jobs associated with emergent knowledge industries such as researching and developing computer software; introducing faster chips for home and business computers; vastly expanding the sciences from new miraculous medications due to gene therapies, new drugs, molecular biology, and physicists' discoveries of ways to raise the productivity of agriculture through genetic modification of organisms; and finding pathways to space exploration. The new occupations, felicitously congealed in Robert Reich's phrase "symbolic analysts," required an educated workforce. To participate in the new economy, displaced workers no less than young people needed education and training. Whereas the "old" workforce needed at best a high-school diploma—or none at all—to qualify for production jobs in the factories and the mills, the "new" workforce needed college credentials and intensive education in math and sciences. To be sure, in the 1980s and 1990s millions of Americans went back to school, as high school became only one step in a prolonged process of education and training.[6]

This rosy picture had the ring of plausibility in the 1990s. It seemed that everywhere, from New York's Silicon Alley to the Palo Alto area's Silicon Valley and the appearance of new enterprises around major and middle-range research universities in the Northeast and Midwest, hundreds of small companies had sprung up to get in on the new economy boom. The research universities were ideal sites because academic computer scientists and engineers became available for consulting and, in many cases, were the proprietors of the software firms. Although some were trying to invent products they could distribute on their own, many were subcontractors to major software companies or had been financed by them to engage in research and development of new products. By the middle of the decade, the growth of the computer-software sector, combined with the completion of the installation of computer systems based on personal computers or networking in a vast array of small companies, created genuine shortages of computer programmers. And the expansion of the health-care industry was providing employment for trained medical personnel of all kinds. Even higher education, in a severe slump since the early 1970s, experienced a mild upswing, especially, but not exclusively, in the science and technology areas.

Major technological innovations know no borders. Even as the United States entered its prosperity bubble, China and India, the largest countries in the developing world, were in different ways undertaking a major historical experiment: They entered the global market both in the production of intermediate-technology consumer products and in knowledge industries. In the 1970s, both the Chinese and Indian governments established extensive educational, scientific, and technological institutions within universities and as independent institutions. From 1990 to 2003, each country's universities and technical institutes graduated hundreds of thousands of scientists, engineers, computer analysts and programmers, and technical professionals. From 2000 to 2003, each graduated some two hundred thousand students in these fields. While the media obsessed about globalization, Indian nationals answered the technical-support lines of computer companies and made marketing calls. The real story was that major U.S. high-tech corporations were outsourcing knowledge work to both countries. Americans have begun to wake up to the reality that Indian and Chinese computer scientists and technicians can perform advanced as well as ordinary research-and-development tasks in computer, laser, and digital technologies for a fifth to a tenth of the salaries of U.S. computer people. Globalization has come not only to material production but also to knowledge work.

But wage cutting and outsourcing of intellectual and manual jobs tell only part of the story. More important, since the 1970s, corporations in the leading industrial sectors—cars and trucks, steel, oil and chemical, electrical, aircraft, machine tools, and textiles—have relentlessly introduced cybernation into the labor process, thereby displacing huge quantities of manual labor. For example, in 1959 there were more than 600,000 workers in the steel industry, including 250,000 in metal fabricating. In 2002 only 150,000 basic steelworkers remained, about 65,000 in the steel-fabricating sector. At the height of World War 2, in 1945, the basic steel industry with a workforce of more than 600,000 produced a little more than seventy-nine million tons. After a brief period of decline, spurred by rising car, building, and appliance industries, steel production increased to its wartime levels without expanding the labor force. Aluminum, plastics, and other lighter materials took their toll on the growth of the industry. Nevertheless by 2001, the industry turned out ninety million tons—about 80 percent of total domestic consumption—with less than a third of the postwar labor force.[7]

In 2003, there were only 107,000 workers in basic steel and 62,000 employees of all kinds in steel fabricating. Worker productivity rose dramatically because steel corporations finally introduced automated and computerized technology, while closing many of the older plants that used the open-hearth or Bessemer processes. Some have argued that the technological tardiness of its largest employer, U.S. Steel, was mainly responsible for the declining position of the U.S. industry in world markets. As the employer of more than half basic steel's labor force, it held a grip on the industry and looked the other way while Japan and Germany were building technologically advanced mills. Instead of plowing a share of profits into modernizing the domestic industry, the corporation became a conglomerate by purchasing Marathon Oil for $700 million and invested in the Japanese steel industry. Now U.S. Steel employs about 30 percent of the total of steel's labor force and has yielded domestic ground to dozens of nonunion small mini-mills that dot the border states. The transformation of the industry from giant to mini-plants is itself a consequence of computerization and other technological innovations.[8]

The auto industry has undergone similar, if less dramatic, changes. In the 1970s, the industry's largest corporation, General Motors, employed 375,000 in its plants and offices. Even as production has increased by a third, its workforce has declined to 265,000. Increased productivity is due to the widespread introduction of just-in-time methods, and to robot and laser technologies. For example, the company's Linden, New Jersey, plant once employed 6,800 workers making Buick, Oldsmobile, and Cadillac cars in two shifts. Technological "downsizing" and product change to SUVs occurred in the late 1980s. Until 2003, the plant's workforce was reduced to 2,600. But the company decided to reduce its stake in the plant's product, the SUV called the Blazer, and eliminating an entire shift, cut the workforce to about 1,000, less than a sixth of 1977 levels. At the same time, GM has systematically closed a dozen assembly and parts plants on the East Coast and the West Coast and reduced by half the workforce in Flint, Michigan, one of its historic flagship cities, while opening plants in rural areas of the South. GM has chosen to eliminate labor in those locations that, in the past, have given it the most trouble on the shop floor, and to reward plants such as Lordstown, Ohio, once a cauldron of rebellion, that have gotten the message that to save jobs, workers should put their collective noses to the grindstone and shelve working-conditions grievances such as speedup and arbitrary individual discharges.

To say "automation," "robotization," and "cybernation" or "computerization" disguises the degree to which post-Fordism is marked by the displacement of "manual" by intellectual labor. In fact, this statement may be refined to note that all labor in the new production regime becomes intellectual. The computerized assembly line only vaguely resembles the older model, when tasks were broken down to the most minute, repetitive level possible— when, for example, a worker in the body shop could put in four welds sixty times an hour, ten hours a day; or on final assembly an entire job is defined as installing two windshield wipers, or putting one or more pieces of trim on the car's body. It is true that the knowledge and the procedures required to make the computerized assembly line are directed by engineers and other technical people, but the operator has herself become a knowledge worker as well. The current line worker often must be able to operate a computer console, recognize signs of malfunction, and sometimes make mathematical calculations.

Enter an automobile- or truck-assembly plant. Relatively few workers operate computer-mediated robots. Some of these eerily resemble a giant skeleton of an arm equipped with fingers to grasp tools and able to move auto parts from one station to another without direct human intervention. In fact, very few hand operations remain in the assembly process, notably in the repair line, where glitches in the assembly process are fixed. Another feature of the new assembly line is that, in contrast to earlier years when dozens of workers were crowded close together, the spaces between work stations are often as long as half a city block. The appearance of the line is a series of machines punctuated by single persons who are significantly diminished in stature.

Here are two additional examples: In 1962 the West Coast International Longshoremen's and Warehousemen's Union (ILWU) signed a far-reaching agreement with the employers' association, the Pacific Maritime Association (PMA). The union, which exercises a high degree of job control in this mostly body-driven industry, agreed after a vigorous internal debate to permit the employers to install containers to pack and lift cargo by machine instead of by hand and back, an innovation that threatened to displace at least two-thirds of the jobs on the Pacific Coast water-fronts, from Puget Sound, Washington, to San Diego. In return, many but not all workers were guaranteed an annual wage equal to their current and future levels, whether they actually worked on any particular day or week or not. A few years later, the East Coast union, the International Longshoremen's Association, signed a parallel agreement providing the guaranteed annual wage for its core members. In the succeeding forty years, dockworkers have benefited from the agreement in two ways: They have shared in the savings that accrue from extensive labor displacement rather than being laid off; and in many cases, they have extended their lives because of the lighter physical burdens. When they work on the docks, they operate machinery and only rarely lift sacks of cargo on their backs. The price of compromise has been to destroy opportunities in this high-wage industry for future generations of workers. The sons and daughters of dockworkers rarely follow their parent onto the waterfront but, if they do not graduate college or university, are obliged to seek jobs in other, usually lower-paid, occupations.[9]

After years of refusal, New York newspaper typographers and printers in the 1970s finally agreed to permit the employers to in-stall highly automated "cold-type"-driven printing processes. A huge aspect of the craft, setting type by hand, was eliminated and most workers were rendered redundant. Now the "typog-rapher" is a computer operator who types in the text like any word processor. None of the members of this highly skilled unionized craft lost their income. Instead they were awarded extended paid "sabbaticals" of six months or more to perform "research" and other nonprinting activities. In time, most of the displaced

workers retired. The permanent legacy of technological displacement in the newspaper industry is that the printing trades have
been severely diminished both in number and in skill, but not in
terms of the volume of production.

The computer, laser, digital, and automation revolutions have
affected every major industry—transportation, communications
and information, wide sections of retail and wholesale trades, and,
of course, manufacturing. For example, since the turn of the twentieth century, the highly volatile apparel and textile industries that
once employed nearly two million people, or 10 percent of the
production labor force of the United States, responded to European competition for cotton fabrics and processed-wool yarn by
shifting their bases from New England and the Middle Atlantic
States to the low-wage U.S. South. For seventy years, textiles remained the economic lifeblood of states such as North Carolina,
South Carolina, Tennessee, and Georgia. Even when fiercely challenged in the 1930s and 1940s and again in the 1970s, employers
were largely successful in fighting off unionization and were able
to operate profitably without large capital investments in labor-
destroying technologies. In the 1970s film *Norma Rae*, viewers
are given an extensive glimpse of the older labor process. A single
operator tended a whole line of electrically powered machines, but
the technology had not changed substantially since 1920. Then,
pressed by global competition in the 1980s and 1990s, the once
technologically sluggish industry undertook a rapid and extensive
program of computer-based technological change. In the 1990s,
multiplant chains such as JP Stevens shuttered old plants or ren-
ovated them to conform to the new lean and mean production
regime. In the late 1990s, union and industry observers were confident that these advances would save the U.S. industry from Chinese and other East Asian competitors. But at the dawn of the
twenty-first century, it has become evident that this hope will not
be fulfilled. China and India have invested heavily in textiles and,

since labor costs still play an important role, have begun to attract U.S. and European capital. In consequence, textile imports to the United States from East Asia and the Middle East, exclusive of apparel, have dramatically increased, and throughout the Southeast, some large employers have closed even the modernized large and medium-sized mills. Those that remain open employ far fewer machine operators because many have been rendered redundant by new technologies. According to the latest figures, there remain about a half-million textile workers in all branches of the industry, including dyeing and finishing.

The startling and largely unexpected change in the nature of the U.S. economy is not so much that traditional industries have been downsized by cybernation and other technologies. These changes were forecast as early as the 1950s when Ford introduced automation to its Cleveland, Ohio, engine plant and industrial engineers and technological planners informed the American people that they should expect more to come. Some, like Robert Theobold, who organized and cowrote a statement by a group of intellectuals, *The Triple Revolution* manifesto, advised that social and industrial policy should begin to address these serious transformations wrought by automation and cybernation. Forecasting that nearly everyone would enjoy more leisure and be free to engage in activities that enhanced their personal development, Theobold and his associates were confident that intelligent planning could forestall mass unemployment. That politicians and labor leaders confined their remedies to providing short-term income supplements to laid-off workers and called on government to promote policies of economic growth on the assumption that growth, rather than proposals such as shorter hours and a guaranteed income, would lead to jobs reveals the degree to which social and political myopia still grips union and official circles. Almost fifty years after the heated debate about the consequences of the technological revolution of our time, not much has changed except the devastation visited on U.S. workers by globalization, and technological change has become an avalanche that has left them with few resources.

The technological optimists who confidently believed that the elimination of manual labor from the industrial workplace would produce only temporary pain have proven to be profoundly short-sighted. What they forgot was not only that design and engineering could be outsourced to China and India, which have been able to graduate tens of thousands of highly qualified architects and de-sign and technical engineers who work for a fraction of salaries required by any Western technical and scientific workforce. More to the point, the nature of the new technologies is that they dis-place intellectual, as well as manual and clerical, labor. While, as I have argued, in many occupations the term "manual" labor no longer describes the competencies and the tasks of the machine op-erator, it is also true that technologies such as computer-aided de-sign and drafting have reduced the labor requirements of civil and mechanical engineering and of many other categories of technosci-entific workers. Retaining the number of scientists and engineers in the wake of technological displacements resulting from inten-sive programming applications that achieve more precision and are self-correcting has proven difficult. Private corporations that employ armies of engineers and scientists, such as General Elec-tric, IBM, and Xerox Corporation, have reduced their professional workforces, and not only by outsourcing their work.[10]

According to the Bureau of Labor Statistics (BLS) there are about two million computer professionals—programmers, systems analysts, and software engineers—in the labor force. Yet according to the BLS:

Employment of programmers [there are about 500,000] . . . is expected to grow much more slowly than that of other computer specialists. With the rapid growth in technology, sophisticated computer software has the capability to write basic code, eliminating the need for more programmers to do this routine work. The consolidation and centralization of systems and applications, developments in packaged software, advances in programming languages and tools, and the growing ability of users to design, write, and implement more of their own programs means that more of the programming functions can be transferred from programmers to other types of workers. Furthermore, as the level of technological innovation and sophistication increases, programmers are likely to face increasing competition from programming businesses overseas, to which much routine work can be contracted out at lower cost.[11]

In 2002, official government forecasts projected more rapid employment growth of software engineers and systems analysts for the period ending 2012. Of course, these forecasts are based on a questionable prediction of steady economic growth. If there is reason to believe that growth rates will, in general, remain sluggish, we can expect only modest gains in computer/professional employment or none at all. But even if the design and analytic end of the field grows as other occupations decline due to the labor-saving consequences of computer work, BLS forecasts changes in the characteristics of the employment relationship in all computer professional occupations—from full-time jobs to more contingent and temporary contracts, from jobs that offer health and pension benefits to work that offers none. In other words, as the industry grows, even by the most optimistic estimates, routine design and programming jobs will be reduced or eliminated, and the higher end of the computer-industry labor force is being converted into contract labor (generously and misleadingly called "self-employed" entrepreneurs, misleading because these professionals work for a single employer). These changes reflect the broad scope of post-Fordist arrangements—more work but fewer jobs.

It is about time we took the scales from our eyes. Military spending, now at record levels, generates fewer jobs than in previous generations because much of the spending is on research-and-development activities rather than production, and the production process is highly computerized. The market is global, which means that when investors receive tax breaks from the federal government, they are likely to put their money in the most profitable sectors of the world economy rather than in the advanced capitalist societies. There is considerable fictitious capital in the various equity markets. But speculation produces few jobs. We are seeing consolidation of companies in retail and wholesale trades, a trend that has already curtailed any but temporary and contingent employment. And laborsaving technologies have had a significant impact on technical and scientific labor.

In the New York Metropolitan Area with its more than fifteen million inhabitants, only three sectors have exhibited job growth in recent years: the predominantly nonprofit health-care sector; education; and the only private-sector industry, tourism and recreation. Although employment in Wall Street and its ancillary financial services has declined, even as institutional investors such as pension funds remain cautious, a small bubble has been created by speculative stock buying, principally by small investors. But these elements are hardly the stuff of which a solid job recovery can be made. What can be done? In Chapter Five, I address this question and show that, if we take a close look at the alternatives, the answers lie in a break, both economic and political, from the past.

FOUR

THE PRICE OF NEOLIBERAL GLOBALIZATION

Adam Smith Comes Roaring Back

I N THE FACE of polls showing that voters ranked the economy as the number-one issue in the presidential election campaign, in April 2004 John Kerry issued a report that charged the Bush administration with plunging the federal government into more than $6.5 trillion in debt. The lion's share of new spending, according to the report, was on "entitlements" such as the Medicare prescription-drug program. According to the report, entitlements would cost $4.9 trillion. On April 6, Kerry said that if elected he would make the "hard choices" of cutting social programs, if necessary, to redress the budget imbalance. But he also promised to create ten million jobs by, among other measures, instituting cuts for 90 percent of taxpayers. The Democratic candidate, accused of liberal sympathies by his opponents, began his economic assault on the administration by taking the position of fiscal conservatism, a stance, as we have seen, borrowed from the Democratic Leadership Council and the Clinton administration during the boom years of the 1990s.

But after more than a year of campaigning, none of the leading Democratic candidates had proposed addressing the nearly intractable structural unemployment of at least ten million people in the labor force by direct job creation. The best the Democrats were able to manage was to try to include a modest rise in the minimum wage in the welfare-reauthorization bill, a strategy designed to embarrass the Republicans and to appease their own base. But mutual allegations aside, since they began from similar premises, the two parties found themselves more in agreement than in disagreement. Having supported the humongous Bush military-spending bill and tax cuts, the main difference was that, on fiscal policy, the Democrats had positioned themselves to the right of President Bush.

One of the main characteristics of neoliberal economics is the view, introduced in the Reagan-Thatcher era, that some tools of economic stimulus are "unthinkable." Economists, politicians, and media are trained to deride "welfare state" proposals as "loony tunes," "spendthrift," and, in any case, objectionable because they would enlarge an already bloated big government. And we all know what is wrong with big government: Under the sign of the welfare state, faceless bureaucrats pry into our personal lives, impose severe restrictions on those who apply for benefits, and perhaps more important, drain our incomes by raising taxes and redistributing them to low-income groups who cannot fuel economic recovery. The fundamental ideal of the neoliberals is, as much as is politically feasible, to confine government to its police functions, at home and abroad. Needless to say, this absurdity is observed more in its breach than in practice, since, as we have noted, those who rail against big government have turned out to be the biggest spenders; moreover, no president has put in place more policies that invade our privacy than George W. Bush. Under the sign of the war against terrorism, the Homeland Security and Patriot Acts have supplied official sanction for shredding individual liberties— and it is not only a question of beefed-up airport or train security. Without a court order, the federal government may now undertake surveillance activities against any suspected citizen, let alone alien resident.

Our leaders justify a huge military establishment on national-security grounds; an expanding domestic police force to wage the wars on drugs and terrorism; and a massive federal highway program to accommodate the fact that, having ritually blocked proposals to expand mass-transit systems, official policy has been to favor the use of automobiles and trucks as our main source of transportation. And few have registered objections to gas-guzzling SUVs, even though it is now generally understood that an oil drought is only decades away. Above all, neoliberals fight recessions with tax cuts and reduced interest rates rather than with public spending. They want to reduce taxes and interest rates to encourage private borrowing and spending. Since 1913 when the Federal Reserve System was established, interest rates are regulated by a semi-autonomous board of governors whose only obligation is to report to Congress. But Congress makes tax law, which means that it has become necessary for conservatives to demonize social spending as well as new taxes. Those politicians who dare cross the line risk political annihilation.

For example, among the reasons many observers believed George W. Bush's father was defeated after a single term in the White House was his widely publicized reversal of a no-tax pledge issued during the 1988 presidential campaign. "No new taxes" has become a bipartisan mantra, the violation of which is said to fatally impair a challenger no less than an officeholder. That George W's tax cuts have plunged the federal treasury into red ink seemed not to have hurt the reelection chances of this wartime president. On the contrary, after three years of a ballooning military budget and stubborn resistance to any new social spending—the White House even cut veterans' benefits—in the service of his reelection, the Bush administration has been willing to darken the red ink by proposing new social programs that it had previously opposed or tried to eliminate. Needless to say, upon taking office for a second term, Bush can be expected, in the name of fiscal prudence, to moderate or even rescind some of these expenditures, just as his pledges to provide $15 billion to fight AIDS in Africa and to fully fund the 2002 No Child Left Behind education program have proven to be largely broken promises. Can we expect Bush to make permanent increased spending on health care, to support increases in jobless benefits and improvements in minimum-wage legislation, when European counterparts such as the Social-Democratic German government and the Center-Right French government are busy trimming these benefits? As in the French case, where the governing Center-Right party suffered defeat in the 2004 regional elections, any concessions a second Bush presidency is likely to make can be attributed to pure expediency.

Unthinkable too is that federal funds should be devoted to creating new jobs, especially those which expand public goods such as schools, housing, public health, recreational facilities, environmental protection, and other services. There are two principle arguments against spending on public goods (except the military and highways, of course). First, public institutions are inefficient; these services are better provided by the private sector because profit and competition are needed incentives to produce better goods and services, and, second, breaking the government monopoly gives individual consumers a wider range of choice among products. Naturally, as in the idea of school vouchers or the Bush Medicare reform, this does not mean that public money might not be made available to private corporations to deliver public services. But if the choice must be made between putting money directly in the pockets of individuals and businesses through tax cuts and adding funds to expand public goods, neoliberals hold the former far more desirable. Presumably, if people have more money, they will spend it and businesses will invest their tax savings directly and indirectly in hiring people. In sum, in neoliberal thinking the private sector should, exclusively, be the source of new jobs.

If we lived in a relatively self-enclosed national economy and if investments were not devoted mainly to labor-saving technologies or outsourcing abroad, this logic would have some credibility, especially in a society dominated by people under the age of forty who never get sick or have accidents on or off the job. The problem is that neoliberal economic assumptions, best enunciated by Adam Smith, are rooted in eighteenth-century conditions. Among those conditions was that England, the birthplace of Smithian economics, was the world's leading mercantilist and colonial power, but its global activities were directed chiefly to procuring raw materials such as cotton for the rising manufacturing sector and tobacco, sugar, and spices for consumption by its growing middle class. Moreover, its economy was dominated by relatively small producers and a high level of market competition. And the public discourse on poverty was limited to keeping the poor from crowding the streets and other public spaces and providing prison houses to train them in the virtues of the work ethic.

This is no longer true in the twenty-first century. We swim in a global economy in which raw materials play an important role but no longer dominate most foreign investments. We are in the midst of a veritable third industrial revolution: The so-called third world—poor agricultural societies located mainly in the southern part of the globe—is in the process of severe shrinkage, if not complete disappearance. The global South is experiencing its own highly compressed economic and social revolution,

where agrarian societies are being transformed into urban industrial societies. Hundreds of millions of peasants have been driven or
have migrated from the land into the cities of Southeast Asia, Latin
America, and Africa, and important agricultural sectors are being
mechanized. They may find employment in construction, factories, and the commodity markets of bulging cities like Shanghai,
Bombay, Macao, Mexico City, and San Paulo. Textiles and textile
products are no longer the principal industries in these cities. San
Paulo has long been a site of heavy-metals fabrication; Mexican
workers drill and refine oil, assemble cars, and produce auto and
appliance parts for North American corporations; and China too
has become a leading petrochemical and appliance, electronics, and
auto manufacturer. Or the migrants arrive to no jobs at all and live
in shantytowns or on the streets and may enter the underground
economy of crime, drugs, and contraband.

In fact, the Chinese economic engine, for example, is much
more complex than usually supposed. Private development, which
has outstripped state enterprises since 1978, has the imprimatur of
the state at every step of the way. The Chinese government pro-
vides the infrastructure, often builds the plants, trains and educates
labor, and builds housing and other facilities for these workers.
Thus private investment is only half the story of the incredible
growth rates reported by the Chinese government. The state has
planned low wages and the vast displacement of agricultural labor
and is responsible for creating a huge industrial reserve army for
the eventual use of private corporations.

Of course, on every continent billions of people still remain
on the land, at least for the time being. But they live in fear that,
however difficult their daily existence, centuries of land tenure will
be destroyed by government edict as in China, falling agricultural
prices as in India and Mexico, the introduction of modern farm
machinery, or the frequent droughts and floods that afflict eroded
soil. In the past decade, more than a half-billion peasants and independent farmers have become landless. Overwhelmingly, they

have gone on a forced march into the urban areas. While the cities are not places of promise, they appear to many the sole alternative to starvation. Which is why, from Chiapas, Mexico, Brazil, and Ecuador to rural China, revolts by peasant organizations and movements of landless workers have dotted the global landscape. They demand agrarian reform, sometimes seize parcels of land from private landowners, and occupy the shrinking acres of public lands and become subsistence farmers. Despite these movements of resistance, the trend toward global urbanization and industrialization seems inexorable. Unless restrictions are placed on the movements of capital, both in the interests of labor and of the environment, in principle no manufacturing job will be secure from the lure of cheaper labor somewhere else in the world and no undeveloped land surface will remain even relatively pristine. Conservation, once the name given to efforts to protect nature from the malign effects of development, would have to be extended to all economic activities, lest the world's population be consigned, as David Harvey has argued, to perpetual dispossession in the service of capital accumulation.[1]

What is new about the current global configuration is that while the gulf between rich and poor widens, fear and trembling has gripped the underlying populations of the most-developed countries as well, particularly the United States. We live in a period when everything seems unhinged, when once-secure jobs are suddenly up for grabs. Apart from having the right to choose the next president and members of Congress, many Americans seem to have lost their collective voice. Enervated by frequent government alerts and warnings of possible terrorist attacks; shocked and then numbed by the avalanche of corporate scandals, many of which are at the expense of both workers and small shareholders; and bewildered by oily, statistical reassurances of economic recovery even as their experience belies such assertions, we have been reduced to bystanders of history and have fewer tools with which to evaluate official reports.

For example, when after two years of an alleged recovery the U.S. Labor Department announced its first monthly substantial gain—308,000 jobs—in four years and the president leaped to the news by claiming his tax-cut initiatives were finally working, the news release upon which the press reports were based forgot to tell us, in detail, what kind of jobs had been created. In fact, of the 308,000 new jobs created in March 2004, 70,000 were in the public and nonprofit sectors (primarily education and health), slightly more than 20 percent of the total, a statistic that indicates how much real job growth still relies on public services. Of the new private-sector jobs, construction, often a seasonal industry, was the biggest gainer at 71,000; 75,000 were in retailing (47,000) and leisure and hospitality (28,000), where low wages predominate. A testament to the ambiguous results of technological and other forms of increased productivity despite increased production, manufacturing failed to add any new jobs at all. The most encouraging signs were in professional and business services, which added 42,000 jobs, although information on how many of these were part-time and in the consultant category was not reported.[2] Days after the Labor Department's news, Bank of America and Sun Systems announced layoffs of fifteen thousand and three thousand respectively. These came on the heels of merger plans by both companies. It is safe to conclude that, apart from construction and a fraction of business services and professional categories, the private sector produced few *good* new jobs.

Recently, my computer was seriously attacked by a virus that disabled its Internet and e-mail features. After attempting to address the problem with my own limited technical resources and abilities, I decided to call my Internet service provider for support. After three sessions with technicians, I was advised to contact the system maker. All four calls were answered by technicians located in offices in Bombay and other cities of India. The technicians were courteous, and in contrast to some Americans I have encountered under similar circumstances, they tried very hard to be helpful. At the end of a full day of frustrating shopping around for assistance, my computer's Internet capacity was not repaired, so I engaged a live technician who made a productive house call and fixed it. During the telephone sessions, I was made aware that my interlocutors frequently needed to consult the manual; they were clearly inexperienced. Of course, if they had succeeded in restoring my service, I could not have cared less. But this anecdote demonstrates the bare fact that Internet providers are extending their outsourcing reach to India, where wages for technical workers as for engineers are a tenth to a fifth of their U.S. counterparts'. In time these workers will gain the experience to match the skills of any U.S. technician. But I wonder what happened to the people in Tennessee and Texas who used to perform these services? Were they downsized, promoted, or assigned to calls from businesses rather than homes?

The point of this story is not to emphasize the evils of outsourcing. Instead I want to call attention to ways in which, in the wake of stagnant computer sales in the first three years of the new century, corporations have managed to sustain their profitability. While the stock markets respond positively to any cost-cutting measures that buttress the price of shares, workers have been left behind. In addition to suffering job destruction and outsourcing, U.S. workers, intellectual as well as manual, are experiencing a long-term assault on their living standards: Wages have lagged behind even the modest inflation rate of about 2.5 percent a year. For the first quarter of 2004, which economists judge as a period of buoyant "recovery" (at least for some profits), total wages rose by 0.6 percent, or an annual rate of 2 percent. Apart from executive compensation, which appears to have retained its high levels during the recession, incomes for many nonsupervisory workers in the private sector, more than 90 percent of whom have no union representation, ranged narrowly between remaining flat (which in real terms is a reduction) and the inflation rate. But some union settlements failed to match the inflation rate as well, so workers actually approved deals that reduced their real wages. For example, a recent contract with the two hundred thousand letter carriers in the U.S. Postal Service, one of the nation's largest employers, awarded workers a first-year bonus that is not included in their base pay, and about 6 percent in salary increases over five years. Similarly, in many recent wage settlements, workers were unable to negotiate any increase at all in the first year of a long-term contract, and modest wage increases were offset by contract provisions that require employees to increase out-of-pocket contributions to health- and pension-insurance programs.

Labor in Retreat

That U.S. workers have experienced a significant reduction in their real wages reflects deep concerns among union and nonunion workers that any militant demands they might make of employers will be met by capital flight or, in the service sectors, intensified outsourcing. As we have already seen, these are not baseless anxieties. The pressure to moderate salary demands and give back substantial features of health and pension benefits corresponds to trends in every industrialized economy of North America and western Europe. Yet the absence of resistance in the United States contrasts sharply with labor union–led mass demonstrations in Italy, France, and Germany against parallel public- and private-sector employer cost-cutting proposals. What accounts for this difference? One factor is that, since the Reagan era, U.S. workers have borne relentless employer attacks at every level: Union settlements gave up hard-won working conditions in a series of concessionary bargains in the 1980s and 1990s; in good times as much as bad times, workers were bludgeoned to accept meager wage increases, a cumulative history that spelled a 25 percent drop in real wages

over the past twenty-five years; and the National Labor Relations
Act, introduced to guarantee workers' organizing rights, has been
reduced to a hollow document, its enforcement provisions consistently eroded or ignored by courts and conservative national
administrations and, more to the point, has been transformed into
employer-rights legislation, bluntly depriving workers and their
unions of their most important weapons, the right to strike in the
public sector, to boycott struck goods, and to conduct sympathy
strikes

It would be unfair and inaccurate to claim that unions have
entirely failed to respond to what is arguably the worst era in
labor relations and workers' power since the 1920s. In 1993,
the AFL-CIO did put up a good fight against NAFTA and has
consistently opposed free-trade legislation that does not provide
genuine wage and working-conditions protection to workers in
trading partners' countries. In this respect, the mass demonstration at the Seattle meeting of the World Trade Organization in
December 1999 was a high point in organized labor's resistance
to a globalizing regime that has produced a torrent of job losses
for U.S. workers and contributed to significant erosion of their
living standards. Union leaders have decried the ineffectiveness
of the labor-relations laws, which prompted a former AFL-CIO
president, Lane Kirkland, to call for their repeal in the 1980s, a
bold maneuver that regrettably has not been followed up by his
successors. Some unions—especially in the service sectors, notably
health care; among low-wage janitors; and in Las Vegas hotels and
higher education—have mounted vigorous organizing campaigns
and saved the labor movement from complete embarrassment during the 1990s, when experts believed that good times would bring
a renewed spurt of organizing, particularly during an ostensibly
prolabor national administration. And, if legislation is part of the
picture, that the Republicans captured Congress in 1994 was surely
a deterrent to union growth. Not only did the environment for

organizing turn sour, but the right-wing administration of the law was even more proemployer than usual. In sum, the combination of antilabor globalization, a conservative political culture, and the consequences of labor-destroying technologies have had devastating effects on workers and their unions.

So far, the account parallels that of many labor experts, liberal economists, and the unions themselves. In this account, workers and their unions are portrayed and portray themselves as victims of an unconscionable employer offensive and conservative national politics. In the main narratives, unions are held virtually blameless for their decline. The problems with this analysis begin with the idea that capital and its representatives can be expected to do something other than address their own crisis of profitability by reducing labor's power in the workplace, at the bargaining table, and in the political arena. But there is no warrant in U.S. history for the assumption of a corporate conscience. Capitalism is an amoral system whose criteria of success are the three components of the bottom line: profits, the subordination of labor, and the imperative of expansion. The only conditions under which employers will raise wages and yield workplace power are when labor is in short supply—in which case governments may temporarily open the gates to immigrant labor to keep wages down—or when workers combine, chiefly through unions and other associations, to force employers and their managers to give ground.

The intensity and scope of mass industrial-union organization during the five years ending in 1938 and the similarly monumental unionizing of public employees from the late 1950s to the early 1970s both indicates the workers' passion to redress decades of grievances against their obdurate employers and is a measure of the severity of the labor-relations regimes under which they were required to labor. Workers and their organizations may call on politicians to support their demands, but the preponderant evidence is that the law intervenes after the fact of upsurge and contestation. As we saw in Chapter Two, laws reflect the strategy of stabilizing class conflict or, as in the instance of the Medicare program enacted by Congress in the turbulent 1960s, of calming what had become a seething movement of retirees demanding coverage after their working years had ended. In short, as in the history of civil rights and abortion rights, labor law usually follows upsurge; rarely does it initiate change.

Although punctuated by infrequent mass strikes such as the great hospital workers' struggle in New York and the monumental emergence of California farm workers' unions in the 1960s and 1970s, the nationwide "wildcat" postal workers strike of 1970–71, and the brilliant 1997 United Parcel Services strike, labor has been on the receiving end of a one-sided class struggle for more than thirty years. I want to argue that employers; antilabor national, state, and local administrations; legislators; and judges have accurately read unions as law-abiding, relatively mild institutions which view themselves at best as pressure groups rather than as a social movement. But many unions do not even rise to the standard of pressure group. Organized labor is today as much a series of insurance companies and tightly knit administrative bureaucracies as democratically organized associations in which members play a vital day-to-day role in governance and policies. Members usually refer to their union as a self-enclosed institution that stands outside their own volition and from which they receive benefits and assistance in solving individual grievances against the employer and contractors of their labor. They often speak of their leaders as they would speak of their employers: distant, powerful, and part of a different and elevated social category. Leaders of the largest unions have become mirror images of the corporate managers with whom they deal. Many union leaders travel in high- and middle-level political and corporate circles and, even as they are obliged to represent their members, have become, de facto, part of the professional/managerial and governing classes. High salaries, generous benefits, and other perks play a role in their growing distance from the rank-and-file members of their respective unions. Consequently, few of them are prepared to take the risks entailed by calling strikes, organizing demonstrations, and forming institutions of political opposition. Their corporatist ideology—they renounce the position of antagonist but in principle always seek accommodation with corporate capital—plays an important role in this reticence, but in the wake of more than a generation of defeats, something else is at play.[3]

National union leaders and a considerable portion of secondary officials have lost confidence that they can win in any major confrontation with government or large employers. Generally, they tend to blame an apathetic membership for their own habitual reluctance to call members to battle on almost any issue. They can cite the lost air-traffic controllers' and the recent Southern California grocery strikes as illustrations of their implied thesis. Nor are they prepared to break restrictive laws in order to advance their demands. Such civil disobedience would have accompanied a putative call for a mass walkout by all labor to protest Reagan's summary dismissal of eleven thousand air-traffic controllers, and for a national solidarity walkout among the hundreds of thousands of unionized supermarket workers, thereby violating federal law that bars sympathy strikes and the provision of their contracts that forbids strikes during the life of the contract. Union leaders have something to fear: the potential loss of the union treasury and with it their jobs and those of the administrative staff, and imprisonment and even legal exclusion from holding union office if demonstrations lead to violence.

Just as New York and California public employees' unions have, in the wake of legislative- and executive-branch demands for productivity, salary, and work-rules concessions, refused to violate antistrike provisions of state public labor-relations laws, so unions that face plant closures and outsourcing of jobs have failed to rally all of labor and the affected communities in protests and political confrontations. Instead, as in a recent case in Michigan where an Electrolux plant located in a one-industry town threatened to move to Mexico unless workers and the local community raised $200 million, they have cooperated with the employer to keep the plant open.[4] When the community came $8 million short of the goal, the company moved anyway. Like many plant closures throughout the industrial heartland, the loss of millions of well-paid union jobs has not provoked many in organized labor to challenge corporate decisions, question their motives, and devise alternatives to accepting the inevitability of defeat. Nor have unions proposed severe penalties against corporations who aggressively take steps to cut costs at the expense of their members and the local communities by plant closures and outsourcing amid layoffs. In fact, when workers and their local unions have chosen to fight rather than submit to the employer, they often discover that national union leaders are hostile to their efforts. The tacit position of today's unions is that management has the "natural" right to dispose of its own property at will and that workers' prerogatives are confined to the provisions of the labor agreement. Since 98 percent of these contracts restrict management rights only under a fairly limited set of conditions, none of which include its right to close or significantly reduce the workforce in the plant, unions tend to remain silent when the company declares its intention to shutter the plant, or they try to engage in ad hoc negotiations to persuade management to reverse its decision by offering substantial economic and shop-floor power concessions.

Collaboration rather than confrontation has become habitual in labor's ranks. In an era when the car industry is undergoing massive restructuring, instead of insisting that U.S. plants be modernized on their traditional sites rather than closed, United Auto Workers leaders have encouraged locals in different plants of the big-three corporations to compete with each other for "product" in order to stave off plant closures. Even as some local unions have thwarted company plans to shut them down through close coop-eration (concessions) in changing work rules, others have not been so lucky. Since the early 1990s, GM and Ford have closed most of their East and West Coast plants and reduced the workforce in dozens of others, while at the same time opening new facilities in the U.S. South and in Latin America, particularly Mexico and Brazil. The union's strategy has been to protect the income of the existing workforce, regardless of these developments. Under the union contract, laid-off workers have the right of transfer to new plants and, during the life of the contract, continue to get paid whether they work or not. And the United Auto Workers union was once a formidable force in restraining industry outsourcing; the contracts today forbid such practices. However, in recent years the union has been so weakened that even in a period of industry growth in 2004, it negotiated a very modest long-term, largely defensive contract even before its expiration. And the auto cor-porations have stepped up their outsourcing to nonunion shops within the United States and to Mexico in violation of the agree-ment. Since, in the interest of preserving its ever-shrinking hold on the domestic labor force, the UAW has openly adopted a pol-icy of working with the auto corporations to save the industry's shrinking market share of the domestic market, it has carefully avoided taking issue with the employers and consequently has not vigorously pursued the outsourcing threat.

The United States has the highest per capita cost of health care, $4,000 a year, of any advanced industrial society. The second highest is Italy at $2,000, and the others are in the $1,200–$1,800 range. The main difference between the United States and other countries is that in this country many components of health care are delivered on a for-profit basis—especially, but not exclusively, prescription drugs—and these costs are largely unregulated. Since life expectancy and other health measures are roughly equal among these societies, there is little warrant for the much repeated claim that U.S. health care is superior to the others. Yet even though they are saddled with health-care and pension costs that can exceed 25 percent of their payrolls and would save considerable money, employers no less than most unions have stubbornly resisted moving to publicly funded programs. Since this opposition cannot be attributed to narrow economic motives, there must be political, cultural, and ideological explanations for the fact that the United States is the only advanced society without national health care. "Creeping socialism" is surely one employer fear; more government surveillance might be another. But why have unions, who have experienced their own health-care crisis, clung to outmoded private plans? What are they afraid of?

Perhaps the most serious immediate problem for workers in both union and nonunion workplaces is the palpable deterioration of private health-insurance programs. This may not be the place to rehearse the long, sad history of the struggle to enact a universal publicly funded health-care program for the American people, but a short summary is necessary. The early New Deal social-security proposals foresaw comprehensive federal insurance that covered unemployment and old age, and eventually a national health-insurance program. But the opposition of the American Medical Association, the U.S. Chamber of Commerce, and the National Association of Manufacturers quickly forced Roosevelt to take universal health care off the table after a congressional defeat in 1939, where it remained until after World War II. Moreover, fearing that a conservative Congress might literally defund old-age insurance if it were included in the general treasury, FDR insisted not only that it be a separate fund but also that it be contributory of both employers and employees, which has proven to be prescient. Organized labor, which by 1946 represented about 30 percent of private-sector workers, became a player in the national political arena, and Harry S Truman's reelection in 1948 prompted the introduction in Congress of a comprehensive health-care measure, the Wagner-Murray-Dingell bill. After a fierce struggle, the bill went down in flames during the first postelection congressional session in 1949, largely because the labor movement was not united behind the bill—many AFL craft unions remained skeptical of government-financed social programs—and the administration gave it half-hearted support in the wake of powerful business opposition.

As it became clear that the Truman administration was more committed to foreign policy than to expanding the New Deal, especially to the struggle to contain the forward march of Communism, unions accepted the discipline on funding new public programs dictated by the budget increases required by putting the country on a permanent war footing and marched steadily toward the creation of a private-welfare state. The most powerful unions in mass-production industries and the strong craft unions swiftly negotiated bilateral agreements with employers to inaugurate what Congress had failed to provide. From 1950 to 1975, unions led the way in the development of private, prepaid health plans, which were funded "in lieu of wages" in the legal definition and were generally employer controlled, which meant that benefits were funneled through for-profit providers such as the large insurance companies. Or, although relying on employer contributions and despite laws requiring employer membership on boards of trustees in industries such as apparel, construction, longshore, and retail trades where small employers predominated, health programs were union administered. Most of the union-sponsored plans provided unlimited full-service hospital care and free doctor visits and prescription drugs for members and their dependents and, in the main, did not require copayments. In the wake of this initiative, hundreds of medium-sized and large nonunion corporations instituted health-insurance programs of varying quality, in part to deter union organization as well as to retain qualified employees. By the end of the 1970s, some 80 percent of all employees in the U.S. workplace were covered by a health plan, and, as Social Security benefits fell behind living standards, more than 60 percent had some form of supplementary pension, often requiring employee as well as employer contributions.

Battered by spiraling premiums caused mainly by rising hospital and drug costs that exceeded the modest inflation rates of the 1990s, union and nonunion health-care programs alike found themselves in big trouble. Unable or unwilling to challenge employers to beef up the funds, many unions conceded substantial money-wage increases in order to maintain their benefits. Among the concessionary bargains in labor agreements over the past fifteen years, many workers are now required to copay for drugs and accept significant deductibles for doctor visits, hospital stays, and surgical procedures, and have seen their dental benefits waste away to practically nothing. Needless to say, as union power receded and employers no longer felt the heat of potential union organization, employees were saddled with even higher costs in unilateral employer-sponsored health care. Typically, these corporations addressed the growing squeeze on profits by reducing their health and pension obligations. Yet for many unions, their self-administered health and pension programs have remained an important political and organizing tool. In an era when many unions are unable to "deliver" to their members generous wage raises and have given ground on many workplace issues, the health and pension plans remain major political assets for retaining membership loyalty to the established administration. And as health care has emerged as a prominent political and economic issue, unions that offer benefits are among the main attractions for workers who lack them, especially in smaller workplaces.

Having negotiated a rich, even if diminishing, private welfare state within the context of collective bargaining, many unions are unwilling to join, let alone lead, the fight for universal publicly funded and administered heath care for all. They have effectively withdrawn from the struggle for public goods except to defend existing entitlements that fall outside the scope of labor agreements, such as Medicare and Social Security. Convention resolutions aside, the labor movement, which shares the pain of increasingly unaffordable private plans, has not supported federally funded single-payer legislation such as that introduced by Representative Jim McDermott, a physician, and his colleagues. Instead, the AFL-CIO and its constituent affiliates have consistently backed Democratic proposals that would award health-care contracts to private-sector insurance companies, some of which are union owned, and to drug companies whose oligopolistic control of prescription-drug prices is largely responsible for plunging many health plans into crisis. Relying on for-profit corporations to provide these services is a formula for unrestrained and ultimately unaffordable costs. The last big push by the Clinton administration to enact such a health-care bonanza for the health industry failed in 1993, the last year of Democratic control over both houses of Congress. Today the situation is far worse.

Despite the steep descent of the U.S. labor movement in numbers as well as industrial power, unions remain the strongest institutional vehicle for the achievement of more economic and social equality. No other voluntary institution has the potential clout to advance the broad interests of working people at every level of the occupational structure, from the working poor to professionals and low-level managers. While other social movements are often resource poor, are committed to a narrow spectrum of social and cultural aims, and are ill equipped, both in ideological and financial terms, to address economic issues because of their class implications, unions have the financial ability to wage electoral, legislative, and organizing campaigns, and their priorities are constrained only by the scales that mar their vision. Unions still have more than sixteen million members and, in some states, are critically important for the Democratic Party's electoral changes and for any possible legislative gains on the economic front. At the national level, organized labor contributes as much as 40 percent of the funds raised by the Democrats; labor-sponsored television and radio ads are indispensable for the party's presidential candidate and for campaigns to save Social Security and Medicare. And in elections, unions field a hefty staff of political professionals and pay for thousands of volunteers for national, congressional, and state campaigns. Finally, even though they represent only 9 percent of the private-sector labor force, union members and their families constitute 24 percent of the total vote in a presidential election. In consequence, what happens in America is still a function, to a substantial degree, of what organized labor is willing—or unwilling—to do.

I would not want to downplay what unions have accomplished in these times of conservative hegemony. Organized labor can claim a large share of the credit for the failure of the neoliberals to completely privatize or to abolish Social Security; for winning and, until recently, protecting Medicare from the steady drumbeat of conservative ideological attacks on its costs, coverage, and administration; and for waging decent but not yet victorious campaigns for raising the minimum wage and against fast-track trade—that is, legislation that confines Congress to voting trade agreements up or down without amendments. But given their social and political weight, the unions also bear considerable responsibility for the growing incomes gap in the United States because they have not challenged the practice of hiding profits in the form of huge executive salaries and perks; for the reduction of real wages in the last quarter century; and, in the light of their political and financial investment in the private-welfare state, for the deterioration of health insurance and the erosion of Social Security, where benefits have sunk below the intention of its framers to provide a reasonable income for retirees.

Millions of retirees are living on Social Security incomes that do not meet federal standards of material comfort, and in many cases, supplementary union-negotiated pensions have remained virtually frozen for many years. In fact, only some of the biggest corporations' pensions, such as those of General Motors, have kept pace with rising living costs. But even GM, the world's largest industrial corporation, has reduced its recent wage offers below the historical level, and to retain benefits, the UAW has gone along. In industries marked by small producers such as apparel, and unions that represent workers in small retail and professional enterprises, the poorly funded welfare funds struggle to maintain benefits, much less increase them. And wages, even in union shops in retail, wholesale, and small manufacturing, have lost ground for years.

The concept of mass strikes for public goods, a practice that is all but routine in some European countries, especially in Italy and France, is so far from the conversation in union circles that to raise the question is tantamount to speaking a foreign language. In this respect, collective-bargaining agreements are not an unvarnished good for workers. They prescribe workers' rights on the shop floor and sharply proscribe the use of the strike weapon to the space after the expiration of the contract. But union leaders persist in extolling the contract as a kind of Magna Carta of workers' rights, even though their members' ability to effectively advance their own interests are shackled by their contracts, which have the force of law. And contrary to widespread skepticism in labor's ranks about the contemporary value of the National Labor Relations Board (NLRB) and the Labor Relations Act itself, while some unions have tried to circumvent the board by demanding recognition on the basis of a check of union membership cards, most continue to use the board's procedures even as they have abandoned efforts to repeal its most onerous provisions. These provisions, the so-called Taft-Hartley amendments to the Labor Relations Act, were designed to seriously weaken labor's power and from an employer perspective have been brilliantly successful, because they have placed the labor movement in a straitjacket from which it shows little inclination to escape. In truth, on the evidence of sharply reduced strike activity since the air-traffic controllers' fi-asco, as well as the virtual absence of mass protests, unions have abandoned direct action as a means to achieve their goals and have largely refused to call upon their rank-and-file members to take militant public action against joblessness or the political attacks on labor's rights, or indeed for a national health-care program. It is safe to say that only sporadically and mainly at the local level has the public face of mass unionism expressed itself in the streets or on the picket line.

Since the Cold War era, which began around 1947–48 when the labor movement purged its ranks of the most militant rank-and-file activists and entered into a very public three-way partner-ship with capital and the state, U.S. unions have surrendered their political and ideological independence. Even before the industrial-union upsurge of the 1930s, labor firebrands were labeled pariahs when not accused of being "Reds" both by government agen-cies and by established union leaders. These epithets were tem-porarily discredited during the rise of the industrial unions, when, as an expedient, some erstwhile antiradicals like Miners president John L. Lewis made alliances with militant leftists, practically the only effective organizers in the movement. But the Cold War wit-nessed a revival of labor antiradicalism amid the transformation of unions into institutions of industrial discipline, class compromise, and adjuncts to U.S. foreign policy. While these characteristic posi-tions have somewhat abated since the collapse of the Soviet Union and the Eastern Bloc, the cultural unconscious survives within the ranks of labor in the form of bureaucratic timidity, paranoia, and frequent repression of rank-and-file reform movements. So even as their backs are against the wall, when not suffused with fear and trembling, the top echelons of union leaders act *as if* they are part of the established power. For the ties that bind unions to the state and to the major corporations have not loosened in this period of retreat. After a brief hiatus during which the AFL-CIO began to reexamine its Cold War relationships to the State Department and to the U.S. intelligence agencies, it has resumed its role as supplicant to government foreign policy. And, playing the role of industry managers—a role which is the least understood—some unions are recipients of federal training funds designed to provide employers with disciplined and qualified workers, especially in service and construction industries. And unions still join with the employers to secure government defense contracts. While there are always good arguments for these forms of collaboration—mainly that they provide jobs—these alliances also compromise the capacity of the labor movement to act outside the political framework of government controls. Moreover, if they worked during the Cold War, collaboration today is a losing strategy, dictated more by habit and fear than by realism.

But the end of the Soviet Union as a rationale for collaboration and tempering labor militancy did not result in a new era of union power and social movement. Despite the best efforts of some union leaders to reverse labor's fortunes by aggressive organizing, the predominate trend within organized labor remained defensive and informed by its collective perception of weakness, a perception which became a self-fulfilling prophecy. The conventional wisdom—eagerly propounded by union leaders and their academic acolytes—explains labor's quiescence: Having lost membership "density" in the private sector (where density designates the proportion of union membership to the labor force), owing mainly to the decline of mass-production jobs, unions cannot hope to make a significant impact on the economic conditions of working people until they regain lost ground by recruiting new members, especially in the sectors of job growth. But this is a long-term mission. For the present, the best strategy is to elect a labor-friendly national administration and Congress that will support organized labor's modest agenda for labor-law reform and extended social benefits.

Surely, since 1995, organizing has become a legitimate priority for a handful of unions who are willing to devote the necessary resources. Some, like the Hotel Employees and Service Employees union, have made impressive inroads in their respective sectors, recruiting tens of thousands of new members in the past decade. But the argument that unions cannot exercise mass power until they have restored their membership strength flies in the face of experiences elsewhere in the world. For example, union membership in France's private sector is slightly less than in the United States, and union density in the French public sector is nearly 40 percent, comparable to their U.S counterparts. Yet French public employees have mounted large demonstrations and one-day strikes against government neoliberal social-welfare policies, truck drivers have blocked highways to win their contract demands, and transportation workers have stopped running busses and trains to underscore their demand that pensions not be reduced or adopt a copay program. In the face of a huge conservative outcry, about which more later, French unions fought for, and won, a nationwide thirty-five-hour week for all employees, and German metalworkers and public employees succeeded in reducing the workweek as well. Similarly, Italian unions of all political stripes have united to stage short-term general strikes against the right-wing government's attempt to roll back entitlements.

Unions have always been at the cutting edge of labor's long struggle to achieve a measure of protection against the vicissitudes of an unstable job market and an oppressive workplace. What has broken down in the last three decades is that working people, nonunion as well as union, have lost their sense of place. What we have termed the "post-Fordist" regime of production and capital accumulation consists, in the first place, in breaking the power of labor to constrain the mobility of capital and to gain a measure of security. Concepts like "flexibility," "globalization," and "technological and organizational innovation" connote that the world has turned upside down. The upshot is that many workers feel as if they are hanging on for dear life. Fragmented by the absence of labor solidarity and of leadership, there has been no period since the early 1930s when organized labor has proven more powerless to resist, or even point the way to opposing, the many-faceted employers' offensive against more than a half-century of workers' gains. But as I have contended, when the labor movement is demobilized, the political and ideological complexion of the entire society shifts sharply to the right, and it is quite independent of what workers, their unions, and the public think they are doing.

Yes, there have been powerful social movements for political and racial equality and economic justice, for sexual freedom and gender equality for women, and for ecological sanity. Each has succeeded in changing the social map of the United States. But with few exceptions, these movements have not joined hands with each other and with labor to address the unfinished agenda of creating conditions for the restoration of our sense of economic well-being and to reverse the incredible power of large corporations whose alliance with the top layers of the political directorate has driven down living standards and created a situation in which authoritarian forms of economic and political rule have become the norm rather than the exception.

It is to this agenda that I now turn.

FIVE

A REAL JOBS AND INCOME PROGRAM

Beyond the Politics of Denial

I N 1936, as the world was enveloped by the Great Depression, John Maynard Keynes published his magisterial treatise *The General Theory of Employment, Interest, and Money*. Keynes noted that the normal operation of modern capitalism could stabilize profits at an acceptable rate of return for a given quantity of capital investment but could not produce full employment. Though Keynes was an economist trained in the classical liberal tradition, he was nevertheless compelled to conclude that government intervention to create public jobs was required to achieve an economy that approximated full employment. This proposition is especially valid in an age when capital investment increasingly takes the form of labor-destroying technologies and national markets have been almost universally superseded by globalization.

Globalization is not new; what is new is that many services, as well
as virtually any kind of material goods, can be produced anywhere.
The unfettered freedom of capital to invest on a global scale means
that U.S.-based transnational corporations can realize substantial
profits by means of foreign investments, while U.S. workers experience increased joblessness and stagnant wages.[1]

Keynes discovered a variant of this disconnect when he advanced a version of underconsumptionism—the idea that depres-
sions and recessions are caused by lack of demand. He argued
that in capitalist societies, "effective" demand would inevitably lag
behind output, thereby discouraging new investment until supply and demand achieved equilibrium. But equilibrium may be
achieved in the balance between output, prices, and profits with-
outfull employment of labor. Essentially, Keynes proposed government job creation to buttress effective demand. Replying to critics
who argued that in the absence of high taxes, budget deficits would
damage the economy in the long run, he quipped, "In the long
run we'll all be dead." He asked his listeners to accept the fact that
capitalism was, like every other economic system, deeply flawed.
In its late stage, it requires periodic bolstering by means of huge
fund injections, the major source of which is the government. This
fact is precisely what is no longer admitted.

We are living through a prolonged period of denial in almost
every corner of public life. Put bluntly, in the past century, except for short periods of dramatic technological innovation such
as the last half of the 1990s, the private sector has proven in-
capable of creating enough jobs to meet the needs of a significant fraction of the labor force. Since the 1920s, massive job
creation has relied primarily on government spending and only
secondarily on the credit system. But since 1980, many goods
purchased through this credit system are produced abroad. This is
why government employment expanded at every level by at least
five times after World War II in a period when the population less

than doubled, and, largely because of the permanent war economy, its investment in productive activities increased by ten times. Even the buoyant housing and consumer markets of the postwar period relied on government action such as government-insured low-interest loans. There is considerable evidence that, as the labor force expands, the gap between private-sector employment and those seeking jobs will grow, not diminish. Business has not hesitated to accept government-generated government contracts, subsidies, tax shelters, deductions, outright gifts, and other breaks. Generally, government largesse is the condition for keeping many corporations afloat. But they perceive no obligation to share their good fortune with the workers. In sum, the free market functions more as a selective ideology and as a boon to corporate America than as a reality.

Keynes advocated deficit spending, if necessary, to achieve job creation and warned that, if capitalists and government officials tarried to take this admittedly distasteful route, they might face Armageddon, especially at a time of mass unemployment in the West. In an era when the Soviet Union was touting the superiority of its system, which it claimed had achieved full employment, and vast movements of the discontented in many countries threatened regime stability from the right as well as from the left, Keynes's unorthodox ideas got a sympathetic hearing in some quarters of the commanding heights of economic and political power. While no Western government was so bold as to fully embrace Keynes's call for massive public spending as an antidote to the inherent tendency of the market to leave a residue of massive unemployment, amid strikes, mass demonstrations against joblessness, and rampant starvation, the New Deal undertook a modest but well-publicized program of public job creation, a policy that reached into the postwar period, albeit in altered and watered-down forms. Conservatives never ceased nipping at the heels of the New Deal and its successors. But critics on the right were compromised by their support of the permanent war economy and the huge federal highway program, the unacknowledged postwar equivalents of Keynesian economic policy.

As we saw in Chapter Three, more than any other postwar president, Ronald Reagan became a full-throated proponent of military Keynesianism and has been matched only by another Republican, George W. Bush. But military spending, which in the era of labor-intensive production was a veritable job machine, has followed the pattern of private and other forms of public spending; investment in computer and other automated technologies produces more goods and services but requires fewer jobs. In contrast to the earlier postwar years, apart from the maintenance of large "peacetime" armed forces, which before 9/11 had become subject to cost-cutting imperatives similar to those for social programs, a high proportion of military spending is devoted to research-and-development activities and to high-tech production regimes which employ relatively few workers. Similarly, in highway construction, workers operate large-scale machinery to perform the once labor-intensive and onerous tasks of land preparation, clearance, and basic foundation construction. Still necessary as an adjunct to early stages of projects and particularly important for finishing operations, the role of manual labor is reduced in contemporary road building. While the billions spent on roads create hundreds of thousands of jobs and, despite free-market foolishness, remain the lifeblood of hundreds of U.S. communities, because of the introduction of labor-saving technology, they get less bang for the buck than they did thirty years ago.

What is missing today is a credible external ideological threat to stimulate new thinking. For, despite the fact of structural unemployment and underemployment, it appears that the wellsprings of creative economic thought have dried up in the West, and the United States is no exception. Our leading economists and conservative politicians remain purveyors of the fiction that good jobs are "just around the corner" and propose new tax cuts for business to accelerate new hiring. That this hiring occurs, but not necessarily in the United States and not at wages that meet the criterion of a decent living standard, is justified as a concomitant of the free market and the necessary price of corporate survival. Put another way, apart from an incipient global justice movement—whose importance should not be underestimated—for all intents and purposes there is no significant opposition to neoliberal economic doctrines and policies, and certainly no public conversation about alternatives. Yet, if the preceding analysis is right, since neoliberalism is indifferent to the fate of working people, the time is long overdue to abandon the project of providing incentives through tax cuts for private corporations.

We urgently need direct public investment to create jobs that expand public goods and a progressive tax system to support the expansion of the only reliable source of jobs: public goods, whether delivered by government or by the government-subsidized non-profit sector. Our material infrastructure is crumbling, particularly in many urban areas, and after some improvement in the 1990s, the physical environment is again dangerous to the public's health: Due to the federal government's relaxation of enforcement and of standards, the air and major bodies of water are badly polluted, and, in consequence, we need to rededicate ourselves to preserving a diminishing marine and wildlife population. Acid rain continues to pollute lakes and rivers; soil erosion and suburban sprawl have narrowed available acres of arable land. And with the growth of the population of seniors, many of whose needs remain unattended, and the neglect by government of the education and health of children, public-sector jobs should be created to address these needs.

Proposals to address structural unemployment by government job creation have always faced two steep hurdles: the seemingly boundless faith in the private sector in free-trade agreements to create jobs, to which nearly all consequential politicians, policy intellectuals, and a sizeable portion of the public have sworn their fealty; and the deep official antipathy to spending for public goods of any kind except for the military and highways. Given these articles of pervasive neoliberal faith, it was somewhat surprising that Congress member Barney Frank, a Massachusetts Democrat, delivered a speech in the House of Representatives in March 2004 declaring: "The normal rule of thumb by which a certain increase in the gross domestic product would produce a concomitant increase in jobs does not appear to apply" to the current economy. Frank went on to argue that the "situation cries out for government job creation. But public pressure is lacking. 'People have so attacked the government,' he [Frank] said, 'that when there is a need for it to help create jobs they cannot recognize a positive role for government.'"[2] Frank cited an important statistic: Every billion dollars in highway construction produces forty-seven thousand jobs. These jobs are directly created by government appropriation. But all the new jobs may not be in direct road building. It addition, if we include the jobs created in the production of machinery, building materials, and concomitant service industries— what Keynes called the "multiplier effect," which he calculated at a ratio of three dollars for each one dollar of public investment— the job numbers are even greater, even if technology and methods of business organization such as self-service retailing reduce the multiplier.

Slightly less than 10 percent of the annual military budget (not counting emergency Iraq funds), $50 billion, would create almost 2.5 million jobs. Needless to say, construction is only an illustration of the kind of public-service jobs that can be created. Jobs could be created to build low-and moderate-rental or limited-equity cooperative housing (where "owners" are obliged to sell their apartments back to the coop rather than offer them for sale in the private market); create a genuine homeland security force; improve our health-care services; expand federal support for child care so that millions of struggling wage-earning parents may keep more of their income and have a safe place to put their kids; expand elementary, secondary, and higher education; provide educational materials to kids without cost to teachers and parents and reduce class size; and expand and enrich after-school programs, which have proven to be among the most effective educational sites. With the official 16.5 percent unemployment rates among sixteen- to twenty-four-year-olds, we might employ hundreds of thousands of young people to clean and maintain our rural, urban, and suburban environments; provide training in occupations such as the building trades, surveying, civil and mechanical engineering technicians, and parks-and-recreation maintenance and management; and offer diploma and degree programs for school dropouts and those who want to continue their education in these and other occupational fields and the liberal arts.

We are in the throes of a housing crisis of monumental proportions. The housing story of the postwar era has been one of federal, state, and local abandonment and betrayal of the brave New Deal public-housing program. It was replaced by a program that used public funds to subsidize private developers by absorbing the costs of land clearance and road access, and encouraging private development of single-household dwellings. In the past twenty years, single-family homes in many regions have become unaffordable for any but affluent buyers and have helped spread suburban sprawl and blight. The situation is so dire that, in search of the American dream of a single-family home, many have put their well-being in jeopardy. Newspapers tell a tale of black and Latino families in New York City who, suffering cramped quarters and skyrocketing rents, have moved out of the city and bought exurban homes two hours or more from their urban workplaces. Not only are the homes badly built and overpriced, but in Pennsylvania's Pocono Mountains, for example, for 20 percent of the buyers the combination of steep mortgages and heavy transportation, day-care, and repair costs have generated foreclosures and the end of their dreams. For many of the rest, it's a long and exhausting day; the American dream has turned into a nightmare. In most cases, both parents must hold jobs to keep up the payments, not only for the house but also for transportation to New York City, and to pay for full-time day care for their children. Working eight hours a day and traveling four hours on a bus five days a week taxes their endurance. Certainly the chronic shortage of housing that people with low and moderate incomes can afford without working themselves into an early grave could be addressed with more funds and policies that earmarked urban land for these purposes. We need to change our current policies of subsidizing private development of housing and of shopping malls and renew our commitment to public housing, creating jobs and alleviating a prime cause of economic hardship at the same time.[3]

Despite the hysteria about national security, our federal budget has failed to provide adequate resources for genuine homeland protection, including workers at airports, seaports, train stations, and other public spaces. The cynicism of the Bush administration was no more evident than in its proliferation of lucrative homeland-security contracts to corporate donors while cheating the workers. Workers in these security jobs are often poorly paid and poorly trained, and there are not enough of them because the federal government is afflicted with the same privatization and cost-cutting mania as the private sector. We could create thousands of federal, state, and local jobs at decent wages to protect our homeland.

Where will we get the funds for creating public jobs and for building new housing, schools, day-care centers, and health facilities, among other public goods? We urgently need to reinstitute a progressive tax system where large corporations and wealthy individuals are required to pay their fair share and no individual or profitable business is exempt from paying taxes. In addition, in the interest of creating these jobs, loopholes for upper-middle-income taxpayers should be closed. And the bloated military budget, much of which neither enhances our security nor is justified if we had a reasonable foreign policy that was not oriented toward empire, could be slashed and reorganized. The savings could help fund a labor-intensive public-service jobs program.

Would this jobs program require a new government institution such as the New Deal Public Works and Works Projects Administrations (PWA and WPA) to administer and coordinate it? Probably, unless the Congress does what it is wont to do in other instances: assign allocation and coordinating functions to the states. But it would be important to stipulate that these are public jobs to expand public goods, and slots should not be created to subsidize wages in the private sector. Right now, huge quantities of federal funds are shoveled into private contractors' pockets. In some cases, contractors hire labor at decent wages, benefits, and union working conditions. In most cases, however, these standards are not observed. In contrast, most public jobs are relatively well paid, contain health and pension benefits, and afford workers union protections.

Sharing the Benefits of Technological Change

In the film comedy *Desk Set* (1955), an efficiency expert, played by Spencer Tracy, is hired by a private corporation to install and train workers to operate a new computer system. Alarmed by the prospect of losing their jobs, the head librarian, played by Katherine Hepburn, and her staff do everything to block the innovation. In the end, the expert convinces the librarians that computerization of most of their functions will not hurt their employment. In fact, the Tracy character did not tell the truth. As in many other occupations, the computer not only reorganized the work but radically reduced the workforce.

If automation produces the same amount with less labor, then logically we ought to be able to work less for the same pay.

In reality, computerization has led to unemployment and under-employment on the one hand, while on the other hand forcing those who do have full-time jobs to work longer and longer hours at less pay. Where did the productivity gains go? To owners and top executives, not to workers. No less than industrial plants, department stores, supermarkets, and government agencies, libraries are stripped almost bare of living labor. Like self-service gas stations, in stores such as Wal-Mart, libraries, and other public facilities rely on the customer's labor as much as on the poorly paid worker. Ours is a time when the eight-hour day and the forty-hour week are on a path to extinction, except for the growing army of involuntary part-time labor that desperately needs more hours but can't find them. If profits have recovered on the backs of labor, not only on long hours and low pay but also via the cost-cutting effects of technology, when will working people share in the benefits of the technological revolution of our time? The promise that automation and cybernation would not only lighten workloads but also provide more time for individual self-development, for participation in public life, and for perform-ing the necessary tasks of care for children and elders, remains unfulfilled after a half century. Most of the benefits of technology have accrued to large corporations and wealthy individuals. As a result, the rich get richer, "middle income" becomes a chimera, and almost everyone works harder for less.

In 1932, a U.S. senator from Alabama, Hugo Black, later a dis-tinguished Supreme Court justice, introduced a bill that would reduce the legal workday to six hours. In the early days of the Roosevelt administration, the Black bill actually passed the Sen-ate but was intercepted on its way to the House of Representa-tives by Roosevelt's labor secretary, Frances Perkins, who believed the bill was much too radical. Due to the administration's pres-sure, the bill died in the House and was resurrected in 1938 as the Wage and Hour Act, which provided for a minimum wage of twenty-five cents an hour (automatically raised to forty cents in 1940), and an eight-hour day, with time-and-a-half pay after forty hours. The congressional intent was to calibrate the minimum wage at 60 percent of the average wage. In 1940, hourly wages averaged seventy-five cents an hour.

Sixty years later, we are on a slippery slope toward the return of the most egregious employment practices of the nineteenth- and early twentieth-century industrializing era. Twenty-one million workers earn wages below the official poverty level and millions more live on the edge of poverty. In many sectors of the economy, the eight-hour day is under siege; Bush has announced his intention to ban overtime pay for federal employees and those working for the federal government's private contractors, and received a temporary setback when Congress balked at the ban's inclusion in various bills. Lacking enforcement of the Wage and Hour Act, many employers require employees to work overtime without additional compensation, on penalty of being fired. But even in the wake of intractable joblessness and the decline of good-paying jobs, there is no public discussion, let alone serious proposals, for shorter hours. And the minimum wage is now a third of the average wage, which exceeds fifteen dollars an hour; attempts to legislate even a modest raise that does not rise to the level of the minimums at their inception have failed in Congress. We need to amend the Wage and Hour Act to provide for overtime pay for work performed after six hours in any day, and after thirty hours a week. We need to immediately raise the federal minimum wage to nine dollars an hour, slightly above the official poverty level, which in almost all metropolitan areas is an unrealistic standard. Like Social Security, it would be adjusted to the Bureau of Labor Statistics Consumer Price Index.

While higher minimum wages and shorter hours—along with job creation—are critical, these measures are not sufficient to address the magnitude of structural unemployment and

underemployment. In winter 2004, 74.6 million Americans between age eighteen and sixty-five were not in, or had left, the
labor force, which indicates they are not looking for paid work.
Of these, some had retired with Social Security and private supplementary pensions. And more than 15 percent were traditional
homemakers. But according to the *New York Times*, more than
half were involuntarily pushed to the sidelines by advancing age,
which restricted their viability in an already crowded job market,
and by the lack of employment opportunities in their regional
and local economies, which discouraged them from participating.
Many men stayed home with the kids while their wives engaged
in wage labor; others were grandparents pressed into day-care service for their grown children; and, of course, millions of young
people had never entered the labor force or were employed only
casually. In an era when 83 percent of women have entered and
remained in the labor force as full- or part-time workers, in part
because only two-paycheck households can keep their collective
heads above water, single parents whose incomes hover around
the official poverty line are drowning. And, as we have seen, in
some urban areas like New York, Detroit, and Chicago, up to half
of black men are chronically unemployed. For these groups there
is no wage.

What to do about the unwaged and the underwaged? On the
assumption that, in the near future, any advance in the minimum
wage is likely to be incremental and therefore inadequate to raise
income levels above the official poverty line, let alone to genuine
comfort levels, America needs a basic-income guarantee. Recall
that such a proposal was on the agenda during President Richard
Nixon's first term in office. His domestic policy advisor, Daniel
Patrick Moynihan, devised a $1,600 per capita annual guarantee.
Duly introduced in Congress in 1969, the measure failed when
welfare-rights and other antipoverty groups attacked it for being inadequate. Thirty-five years later, compounding and taking

inflation into account, the Moynihan plan is worth $12,000—about $6 an hour, still substantially below the official poverty line. But the basic income could be seen as a supplement to income from earned wages. It could be enacted as a negative income tax, where a standard is established against actual income. The difference between the two would define the public commitment. It is time to revive the concept of a basic guaranteed income for all Americans.

A Reasonable Trade Policy

The last major national economic debate occurred in 1993, in advance of the North American Free Trade Agreement (NAFTA). The proposal establishes a free-trade zone among the three North American nations: the United States, Mexico, and Canada. Unions and environmentalists characterized the proposal as an invitation to corporations to abandon the United States or to engage in extensive outsourcing, which inevitably would result in a job drain. After waffling on whether to support this fundamental alteration in the historic right of government to impose tariffs and quotas to protect domestic jobs and industries, President Bill Clinton placed the full weight of his administration behind the measure. The AFL-CIO led a coalition of unions, environmentalists, and civil-rights groups to oppose it. In the end, Clinton negotiated some mild environmental and labor protections to be included within the treaty, but organized labor, in one of its rare acts of courage and aggressiveness, characterized these concessions as window dressing and almost defeated the bill. By the time Clinton left office in January 2001, by some estimates more than four hundred thousand U.S. jobs had been lost to Mexico and, to a lesser extent, Canada. While many activists in Mexico welcomed NAFTA as a boon to that country's economic development, their approval was short-lived. Ten years later, the once-booming region around Juarez bordering the United States, which as a recipient of U.S. capital investment made auto parts, appliances, apparel, and many other goods, found its wage rates of a fifth of U.S. wages too expensive. Around the year 2000, thousands of jobs from these factories, known as maquiladoras, began to migrate from Mexico to East Asia, where wage rates were even lower.

Six years later, a 1999 Seattle meeting of the World Trade Organization (WT0)—the agency responsible for policing trade agreements—was greeted by a demonstration by fifty thousand steel, longshore, and service employees, union members, feminists, antisweatshop groups, and environmentalists. Not merely a march and rally, the demonstration was marked by civil disobedience and battles with police. But the event, which was heard around the world, became the occasion for the emergence of an anticorporate global justice movement that was followed by mass outpourings of new opposition in Washington, Quebec, Genoa, and Madrid and the formation of the World Social Forum, which has brought hundreds of thousands of activists to Porto Alegre, Brazil; Saint Denis, a Paris industrial suburb; and India. As a result of these struggles, questions of trade have now become crucial political issues in almost every country. In each, the debate takes somewhat different forms.

In the United States, the 2004 election brought to a head seething resentment by workers and dozens of industrial communities against the escalation of outsourcing, the extension of the NAFTA framework to what the Bush administration terms the Free Trade of the Americas Agreement (FTAA) to thirty-three countries, and the virtual free-trade relations this country has forged with China and other newly emerging industrializing nations of East Asia. U.S. workers, not only in the Northeast but also in the industrial-heartland states of Ohio, Missouri, and Michigan, have witnessed the exodus of hundreds of thousands of jobs since the mid-1990s, and the pace has accelerated since 2000. Clearly, even though the national Democratic Party leadership and the Republicans are united on the project of removing all trade barriers to the free global movement of capital, a new trade policy is urgently needed.

Every trade agreement should contain the following provisions:

- Strictly enforced environmental and labor protections for both U.S. workers and workers in the recipient countries. These agreements should specify standards: wages, working conditions, and the right of workers to organize unions of their own choosing. And no investment should be sanctioned without obtaining an environmental-impact study to determine effects of industrialization on air, water, land, and other public resources.
- Labor, environmental, and citizens groups should be at the table in the drafting of all agreements and should constitute an independent governing board for their administration.
- Commodities sold in the United States should be subject to a "domestic-content" standard—that is, a definite proportion of all goods should be made in the United States, and waivers to this rule should be subject to approval by the independent governing board.
- Just like most wage and salary earners, most businesses should be required to pay taxes, the avoidance of which may result in the loss of their corporate charters. Corporations that register offshore must be required to pay U.S. taxes. Those who avoid such taxes should lose their right to sell their goods and services in this country. (Of all U.S. corporations, 60 percent failed to pay taxes in 2003. Many of them were registered in another country, usually a Caribbean site; others simply took advantage of gaping loopholes in U.S. tax law.)

This is not the traditional tariff and quota protectionism. Yes, there should be job and environmental protections built into every trade agreement. And corporations engaged in global commerce should be subject to regulation. The point of these proposals is to raise global living standards, both in terms of income and with respect to the environment. And they are aimed at rescinding the off-shore and tax-dodging corporate swindle that has deprived the U.S. Treasury of trillions of dollars and U.S. workers of more than a million jobs in the last decade.

In the last analysis, the jobs, income security, and ecological protection of people in the United States depend not on protectionism but on raising the living and working conditions of the entire global population. Only when poverty, hunger, and disease are seen as global issues can Americans have any freedom from fear. But international solidarity cannot be forged on the basis of a zero-sum game. The gain of capital cannot be purchased at the price of labor's losses. Nor should one group of workers gain at the expense of another. Since 1886, by law and judicial decisions, the corporate form of business organization has the privilege of limited liability because corporations are treated as individuals and have individuals' rights. Paradoxically, they are considered persons. In return, according to the terms and conditions of this privileged status, they have obligations to advance the public good. But since the mid-1880s, corporations have regarded themselves as sovereign actors with the uninhibited sacred right to abandon communities, often leaving them completely bereft, and to transgress national borders. For these reasons, we need to re-regulate the behavior of corporate capital, to democratize trade and global political relations, and to significantly revise the law with respect to the rights and responsibilities of corporations—especially, to make corporate officials individually responsible for malfeasance such as misusing employee-pension funds, misstating profits and losses, and other abuses.

Obstacles to a Reasonable Policy

If my program sees the light of day, we may expect to hear at least three different objections. First, in this global economy, we have already experienced capital flight. Raising wages and shortening hours, raising taxes to pay for a guaranteed income and public job creation, and restricting corporate "rights" would accelerate this trend. Second, small businesses, whose profit margins are thin, would be hurt; many businesses are likely to fail. And third, America's already eroded competitive position in the global economy would experience a catastrophic fall. Taken together, these tendencies would force employers to undertake even more draconian laborsaving measures and would tempt them to flagrantly disregard existing protective legislation. In short, if unemployment is growing in a relatively low-wage, low-tax, largely unregulated economy, then raising wages, lowering hours, and otherwise increasing the costs of doing business will produce even more joblessness.

Yet other countries have taken similar measures without the sky falling. It is an open secret, except to most Americans, that the U.S. minimum wage lags behind that of most advanced industrial societies. For example, while Germany has no national minimum wage, it has established, by law, industry minimums: In West Germany, based on April 2004 exchange rates, the minimum wage for construction workers is 12.3 Euros an hour (about $15), and in East Germany, the minimum is 9.5 Euros (about $12); for agricultural laborers, a relatively unskilled occupation in a traditionally low-wage sector, the minimum of 6.4 Euros is equivalent to more than $7.50 an hour. The French have a national minimum wage that is currently 1,200 Euros a month (about $1,500, or about $11 an hour on the basis of the thirty-five-hour week). The German metalworkers' union raised the issue of shorter hours in the early 1990s and conducted a powerful national campaign to force employers to meet their demand for a thirty-five-hour week but fell short of success. Yet, after a national strike, public employees reduced their working hours from 40 to 38.5 hours. And amid conservative and employer warnings that the economy would plunge into chaos if shorter hours were enacted, the French National Assembly passed thirty-five-hour legislation, and at last sighting, the economy is still afloat. Since the thirty-five-hour week was introduced, with no loss in pay, gross domestic product and worker productivity have risen. Many European countries provide full child-care services and free health care and have a genuine public-housing program. True, citizens and corporations pay higher taxes than in the United States for these services. But their commitments are different: In the United States, public policy favors private gain; in Canada and Western Europe until recently, public goods have high social value. Since the United States often resembles a huge social and political island removed from the rest of the world in most respects except investment and trade, comparative knowledge seems to have made almost no difference in our national political life.

Still, the neoliberal objections can't be ignored. Absent a global movement to raise living standards, since the 1970s corporate America has displayed a degree of ruthlessness in the pursuit of its interests unknown since the Gilded Age, when the robber barons plundered the natural environment, exterminated Native American nations, and mercilessly exploited wage labor, even as it industrialized a once agricultural society. General Electric, among America's largest corporations, has laid waste nearly a dozen northeastern cities it once dominated, and U.S. Steel's anti-ecological treatment of western Pennsylvania and eastern Ohio was no less brutal. One need only visit the Detroit area, the former hub of the auto industry, to witness the devastation inflicted on this industrial city by the auto industry. Michigan remains an important auto center, but since the 1960s, it has become a poster child for the deleterious effects of capital flight. Under present conditions, there is no reason to believe that these and many other leading corporations will respond to new wage-and-hour legislation restrictions in any manner other than their historical proclivity to slash and burn.

If such reforms were introduced in Congress, let alone implemented, we could expect a concerted campaign by the Right and by the representatives of capital to launch massive propaganda directed to intensifying the fear and foreboding of working Americans. Facing this sobering reality, we must ask ourselves a fundamental question: What is the status of freedom, if the price of a job is to permanently subordinate ourselves to our rulers? Can we trust big business to toe a patriotic line of corporate responsibility to American workers, their children, and their communities? And how must we evaluate a political system whose loyalty to capital supersedes its responsibility to the citizenry? Further, in the face of high anxiety, popular quiescence, and the absence of political and social constraints, must we accept the divine right of capital when corporations have arrogated to themselves almost total economic sovereignty and have brought the political system to heel? The stakes in submitting to threats and intimidation are nothing less than the permanent domination of capital over every aspect of our lives. If we refuse to have a public discussion about what can be done to address our country's economic problems and instead continue to bow to the cockeyed realism that has kept us until now from taking aggressive public action, we might well ask, What is the meaning of democracy in America? Given the virtual absence of a political opposition, is the act of voting simply a plebiscite to ratify the existing state of affairs, regardless of which political party prevails? Or does democracy entail public debate among competing ideas about what should be done?

The basic assumptions of this program are that the free market is a fiction and that free trade is both propaganda and a series of practices that widen class inequality, create more human misery, and subvert democracy. We may paraphrase A. J. Liebling's famous remark that "the press is free for those who own one." Free markets are free for those who dominate them. The interests and needs of the American people require urgent attention. Since neither major political party seems ready to advocate the necessary steps, equally urgent is the task of crafting new political vehicles for addressing them.

NOTES

PREFACE

1. Stanley Aronowitz and William DiFazio, *The Jobless Future: Sci-tech and the Future of Work* (Minneapolis: University of Minnesota Press, 1994).
2. Robert Reich, *The Work of Nations* (Boston: Addison Wesley, 1991).
3. John Kenneth Galbraith, *The Affluent Society* (Boston: Houghton Mifflin, 1998).

INTRODUCTION

1. Steven Greenhouse, "Looks Like a Recovery, Feels Like a Recession," *New York Times*, September 1, 2003.
2. "Jobs in an Evolving Economy: To the Lowest Bidder Goes the Lowest Pay—U.S. Towns Bear the Brunt of Jobs Loss to Mexico and Asia," *Idaho Statesman*, December 15, 2003.
3. Louis Uchitelle, "Employers Balk at New Hiring Despite Growth," *New York Times*, December 6, 2003.
4. Paul Krugman, "Our So-Called Boom," *New York Times*, December 30, 2003.
5. Floyd Norris, "Grasping at the Statistics on the Self-Employed," *New York Times*, December 6, 2003. Bernstein's quote is from this article.
6. Stephanie Kang and Amy Merrick, "Retailers Blink in Holiday Standoff," *Wall Street Journal*, December 15, 2003.

7. Edmund Andrews, "Deficit Study Disputes Role of Economy," *New York Times*, March 16, 2004.

8. Employment Policies Institute Report, "Where the Jobs Aren't: Local Unemployment Spreads," Washington, D.C., July 2002.

9. Kathleen Barker and Kathleen Christiansen, *Contingent Work: American Employment Relations in Transition* (Ithaca: Cornell University Press, 1998).

10. "Job Market," *New York Times*, January 25, 2004.

CHAPTER ONE

1. Paul Krugman, *The Great Unraveling* (New York: W.W. Norton, 2003), xx.

2. Eric Foner, *Reconstruction: America's Unfinished Revolution, 1863–1877* (New York: Harper and Row, 1988).

3. Lawrence Goodwyn, *Democratic Promise* (New York: Oxford University Press, 1976).

4. Bernard DeVoto, *The Year of Decision: 1846* (New York: St. Martin's Griffin, 2000); Richard Drinnon, *Facing West: The Metaphysics of Indian-Hating and Empire-Building* (New York: New American Library, 1980).

5. See William Appleman Williams, *The Contours of American History* (Chicago: Quadrangle Books, 1961).

6. For a contrary view, see Robert William Fogel, *Railroads and Economic Growth* (Baltimore: Johns Hopkins University Press, 1964).

7. Matthew Josephson, *The Robber Barons* (New York: Harcourt, 1992 [1940]). Nick Salvatore, *Eugene V. Debs: Citizen and Socialist* (Urbana: University of Illinois Press, 1982).

8. Milton Friedman, *Capitalism and Freedom* (Chicago: University of Chicago Press, 1961).

9. Lewis Corey, *The Decline of American Capitalism* (New York: Covici Friede, 1934).

10. Robert McElvane, *The Great Depression: America, 1929–1941* (New York: Times Books, 1984).

11. Arthur Altmeyer, *The Formative Years of Social Security* (Madison: University of Wisconsin Press, 1966), 11.

12. Ibid., 116.

13. John Hoerr, *And the Wolf Finally Came* (Pittsburgh: University of Pittsburgh Press, 1988).

14. Martin Sklar, "On the Proletarian Revolution and the End of Political-Economic Society," *Radical America*, May 1969, 1–39.

CHAPTER TWO

1. Eduardo Porter, "The Bright Side of Sending Jobs Overseas," New York Times, February 15, 2004.

2. Charles L. Heartherly, ed., *Mandate for Leadership: Policy Management in a Conservative Administration* (Washington, D.C.: Heritage Foundation, 1981).

3. Ibid., 248–49.

4. Randy Martin, *The Financialization of Everyday Life* (Philadelphia: Temple University Press, 2003).

5. Helen Lachs Ginsburg and William Ayres, "Employment Statistics: Let's Tell the Whole Story," National Jobs for All Coalition report, March 2004.

6. Barry Bluestone and Bennett Harrison, *The Deindustrialization of America* (New York: Basic Books, 1982), 6–7, 35.

7. Aronowitz and DiFazio, *The Jobless Future.*

8. David Lilienthal, *Big Business: A New Era* (New York: Arno Press, 1952).

9. Louis Uchitelle and N. R. Kleinfeld, "The Price of Job Loss," in *The Downsizing of America*, a *New York Times* Special Report (New York: Three Rivers Press, 1986), 17.

10. Ibid.

11. Michael Harrington, *The Other America* (New York: Scribners, 1962).

CHAPTER THREE

1. Christopher Caudwell, "The Democrats Can't Take Comfort in the Economy," *Financial Times*, March 30, 2004.

2. Mark Levitan, *A Crisis of Black Male Employment: Unemployment and Joblessness in New York City, 2003.* Community Service Society Annual Report, February 28, 2004.

3. Calculation is based on an analysis of census data performed by the National Jobs for All Coalition. The Economic Policy Institute (EPI) reports 2.4 million "missing" workers who, if counted as unemployed, would boost the jobless rate to 7.7 percent. EPI seems to accept the official government method of counting involuntary part-time workers as fully employed, discounts the category of underemployment, and ignores the huge prison population. None of the statistical accounts by liberal or conservative policy institutions try to evaluate the impact of the more than 10.5 million full-time college students on the unemployment rate. In addition there are some 5 million part-time students. Of course, many in both categories are engaged in part- or full-time wage labor. Many, if not most, are full-time students who if required to enter the labor force would swell the ranks of the unemployed.

4. James Surowiecki, "Lies, Damn Lies, and Statistics," *New Yorker*, April 14, 2004.

5. Stanley Aronowitz, *Food, Shelter, and the American Dream* (New York: Seabury, 1974).

6. Reich, *The Work of Nations.*

7. U.S. Department of Labor, Bureau of Labor Statistics, "Out of the Steel Industry" (Washington, D.C.: U.S. Department of Labor, Bureau of Labor Statistics, spring 2004).

8. Hoerr, *And the Wolf Finally Came.*

9. William DiFazio, *Longshoremen* (South Hadley, Mass.: Bergin and Garvey, 1984).

10. Aronowitz and DiFazio, *The Jobless Future.*

11. U.S. Department of Labor, Bureau of Labor Statistics, *Occupational Outlook Handbook* (Washington, D.C.: U.S. Department of Labor, Bureau of Labor Statistics, April 2004).

CHAPTER FOUR

1. David Harvey, *The New Imperialism* (London and New York: Verso, 2004).
2. U.S. Department of Labor, Bureau of Labor Statistics, "Employment Situation Survey" (Washington, D.C.: U.S. Department of Labor, Bureau of Labor Statistics, April 2004).
3. Stanley Aronowitz, *False Promises* (Durham, N.C.: Duke University Press, 1992), chap. 4, and *How Class Works* (New Haven, Conn.: Yale University Press, 2003).
4. The comments on the closing of this Greenville, Michigan, plant are extensive in both the daily press and other sources; 2,700 workers lost their jobs, but the company cited "good common sense" as the reason for taking the action.

CHAPTER FIVE

1. John Maynard Keynes, *The General Theory of Employment, Interest, and Money* (London: Macmillan, 1936; New York: Harcourt, Brace and World, 1964).
2. Barney Frank quoted in Louis Uchitelle, "Maybe It's Time for Another New Deal?" *New York Times*, April 11, 2004.
3. Michael Moss and Andrew Jacobs, "Blue Skies and Green Yards, All Lost to Red Ink," *New York Times*, April 11, 2004.

INDEX